Praise for

I have watched God's grace over the past couple of years and move a place of hurt, disappointment, and despair to a place in God that has allowed her to remove every mask that held her captive to her past. You will be truly blessed beyond measure as you read and share Frances' journey *From Despair to Deliverance,* and you will literally be delivered from the hurting places that you have been masking for years. This book will help you to peel away every *Mask* that you used to hide from the public for many years. I encourage you to allow the Word of God, as it is ministered to you by Frances, to give you beauty for ashes and the oil of joy for mourning and the garment of praise for the spirit of heaviness as you are *delivered; unveiling the lies of the enemy. Celebrate today* the freedom in Christ that His blood has made available for us. I am excited for your *Deliverance and Unveiling...HALLELUAH!!!*

Psalms 147:3 (Amplified) He heals the brokenhearted and binds up their wounds [curing their pains and their sorrows].

Rev. Vernetta Y. Meyers
(Author of *Good Morning, Co-Workers; Your Daily Bread*)

FROM DESPAIR
TO DELIVERANCE

From Despair to Deliverance

Unveiling the Mask

Frances A. Outlaw

Tate Publishing & Enterprises

Published by Tate Publishing & Enterprises, LLC
127 E. Trade Center Terrace | Mustang, Oklahoma 73064 USA
1.888.361.9473 | www.tatepublishing.com

Tate Publishing is committed to excellence in the publishing industry. The company reflects the philosophy established by the founders, based on Psalm 68:11,
"The Lord gave the word and great was the company of those who published it."

Book design copyright © 2008 by Tate Publishing, LLC. All rights reserved.
Cover design by Nathan Harmony
Interior design by Lynly D. Taylor

Published in the United States of America

ISBN: 978-1-60604-662-3
1. Biography & Autobiography: Personal Memoirs
2. Inspiration: Personal Memoirs

08.11.10

This book is dedicated to the loving memory of my brother Aaron "Eric" Outlaw, a man who became my hero long before I knew I needed one.

ACKNOWLEDGEMENTS

First of all I would like to thank God, who is the head of my life, for placing in me His word and the tenacity to see this project through no matter what the cost.

To my four beautiful children Demetrias, Diara, Devon, and Douglas, thank you for bringing meaning to my life and giving me more joy than any mother could ever imagine. Thank you for believing in me even when I didn't believe in myself. You all have taught me the meaning of unconditional love.

To my parents Willie and Elaine Capehart and my nine living siblings, Dyron, Juanita, Doris, Towanda, Rhonda, Cheryl, Sylvia, Benita, and Trevor. I could not be prouder to be a part of such a talented and loving family.

To my spiritual leaders, Bishop Richard B. Peoples and Dr. Janice Peoples. You will never know how much your teachings and the examples you've shown me through watching your walk with Christ has changed my life. Thanks for becoming my role models for an anointed walk with Christ.

To Rosalyn Cadle, thank you for taking on the exhausting task of editing my book. You made sure that my voice and my unique personality were not lost in the process.

To my "*vision circle*": Cheryl Jones-Butler, Jackie Lee, Carmen Clark, Minister Vernetta Meyers, Janice Rice, Yvonne Young, Janiece Blankenship, Faith Lashley, Sabrina Tutt, Sandra Carter-Cunningham, Yvonne Daniels, and Priscilla Smart-Mason, thank you all for continually speaking words of encouragement into my life as I struggled through the emotional rollercoaster ride writing this book. You all saw God's vision for this book and encouraged me to believe what God had destined for my life. To this awesome group of Virtuous Women I say, "Sore high Mighty Women of God, sore high!"

A special thanks goes out to Jackie Lee for allowing God to use her to constantly speak into my life. You challenged my thought process, my faith, and my gift daily to help pull out of me what God has put inside of me. You never ceased to tell me that God placed you in my life to remind me daily what an awesome, anointed woman I am. Thank you for helping me realize it for myself.

To the Members of Faith Outreach Christian Life Center, thank you all for welcoming my family and I with such loving arms. I pray that our church forever keeps that welcoming spirit.

I pray that this book will make you all proud.

CONTENTS

FOREWORD

Frances A. "Lisa" Outlaw, through the God inspired gift of journaling, has produced a direct and transparent manuscript unveiling and revealing in intimate detail the many physical and emotional hurts, battles, and struggles with life's situations that plagued and controlled her life for a season. Lisa acknowledges that surrendering her life to Jesus Christ put her on the path to deliverance, and through her diligence to daily study and meditation on God's Word, she has been as a result able to bring up and bring out all the negative feelings and emotions that brought her from a life of despair to the healing and delivering light and power of the Word of God.

I believe that those who read Lisa's manuscript will be able to identify and receive God's healing and deliverance from many of their own personal struggles as well. Lisa, through journaling, has been able to successfully give a living testimony of how God can take a life of brokenness and despair and bring restoration, wholeness, and peace. Lisa is now able to see and fulfill God's plan and purpose for her life in this season, by giving testimony of how her life was gloriously changed. She found healing and deliverance in

His name, joy in His presence, peace under the shadow of His arms, and love in His bosom. I applaud you, woman of God. Continue to allow God's leading in all your future endeavors.

2 Corinthians 4:6–9
Bishop Richard B. Peoples
Pastor of Faith Outreach Christian Life Center
Augusta, GA.

FRANCES A. OUTLAW

PREFACE

What happens when you find your life in total despair? How do you put into words what you feel when all that you know is suddenly questioned? Throughout your life, situations will occur that will have you questioning yourself and even God. There will be situations that you will have control over and then there will be those times when you have absolutely none.

Take a trip with me through the despair of my life and see how giving my life to Christ was the beginning of my deliverance. While reading this book, hopefully you will find something in it that you yourself can identify with that will help you begin your own healing process.

Most people will only be able to identify with one or two of the writings, but I identify with them all because they are all situations that I have lived through. My life is a testimony of how God can take a completely broken life and put it back together again. Even as I was writing this book my healing was taking place. Things I thought I had let die, past and present, were not dead, but just buried. Healing does not begin until you let it out. It is time for you to release the things of old and walk through new doors.

Before you turn this page you must first let go of all of your inhibitions and doubts. Free your mind of all the negativity and prepare yourself for a self-evaluation. Ask yourself the following questions as you read this book: Can I identify with any of the writings? Have I truly healed from those feelings? How do I obtain healing and deliverance from those feelings? How do I gain control of my life again?

For those of you that find after reading this book, that none of the writings apply to you, ask yourself if there is anyone that you may know to whom this book may be of some help? If you can think of anyone, be a blessing and share the book. There is something in this book for every one that has gone through some form of despair in his or her life. They may not be able to express how they feel, but they can find something in this book that they can give to someone and say, *"This is me"*.

God has an answer to every situation you have faced or will face in your life. Let God be your Deliverer. All you have to do is give Him the opportunity to come into your life. This is your chance for God to show you that, "He Is". Find your way out of despair into a life of deliverance through the Word of God. He will take your life *"From Despair To Deliverance"*.

He healeth the broken in heart, and bindeth up their wounds.

(Psalms 147:3, kjv)

The Spirit of the Lord is upon me, because he hath anointed me to preach the gospel to the poor; he hath sent me to heal the brokenhearted, to preach deliverance to the captives, and recovering of sight to the blind, to set at liberty them that are bruised. To preach the acceptable year of the Lord.

(Luke 4:18–19, kjv)

PURPOSE

My purpose has finally been revealed: To minister the Word of God to those who need to heal. Healing from their broken heartedness. Healing for their wounded souls. Healing from the issues of everyday life that have never been told. Telling them about God's goodness and His grace and how He brought me through. Letting them know that He is the only way to a breakthrough. Sharing my life of despair through inspirational writings. Showing them how He performs.

My life was a struggle. It was a daily battle. God came to tell me that my salvation was all that mattered. Broken and beaten, He did not care. Baggage in hand with even more to bear. All the pain and suffering was for a reason. He had a plan and a purpose for this very season. To fulfill my purpose here on earth by giving testimony of how my life was changed. How I found healing in His name. Joy in His presence. Peace under the shadows of His arms. Love in His bosom. *"For all have sinned, and come short of His glory."* All that He asked me to do was proclaim Him as Lord and Savior over my life. Believing in my heart that He raised Jesus from the dead. Surrendering my all to Him by placing my life in His hands.

Many people will ask, "Why would she put her life on display for the whole world to see?" There will be those that will make hurtful statements and ridicule the things that I have confided in this book. To those people I can say, "You have already missed the message." My life is not my own, it belongs to Jesus Christ and I am here to do His will.

> And we know that all things work together for good to them that love God, to them who are the called according to his purpose. For whom he did foreknow, he also did predestinate to be conformed to the image of his Son, that he might be the firstborn among many brethren. Moreover whom he did predestinate, them he also called: and whom he called, them he also justified: and whom he justified, them he also glorified. What shall we then say to these things? If God be for us, who can be against us? He that spared not his own Son, but delivered him up for us all, how shall he not with him also freely give us all things? Who shall lay any thing to the charge of God's elect? It is God that justifieth.

> (Romans 8:28–33, kjv)

My life is a testimony of how God has brought me

through some of the most horrifying, desperate, and lonely times in my life. My story is for that one that may be hurting, but who can't seem to find their way back to peace. It's a message of hope for anyone who feels that they have a noose around their neck waiting to take that last yank to end it all. This is for that individual whose childhood was snatched from them unwillingly. This is encouragement for that person whose life is in shambles and has already, in secret, made the decision to give up before their life even begins. I pray that this book will reach them all in time.

For one moment forget that this book is about me. Think about what any one of your loved ones might be going through or have gone through. Can you think of anyone who may have shut him or herself off for no apparent reason? Could it possibly be that there is something deeper going on with them, more than them being a loner, possibly upset or shy? The testimonies in this book were written to bear witness to the goodness, mercy, and grace of our Lord and Savior Jesus Christ. Its purpose is to remind the world that if they would diligently seek Him in all things pertaining to life He will give them the desires of their heart. "Delight thyself also in the Lord; and he shall give thee the desires of thine heart. Commit thy way unto the Lord; trust also in him; and he shall bring it to pass." (Psalm 37:4–5, KJV)

God has given each and everyone of us a purpose. Do you know what your purpose is? Have you taken the time to get to know God so that He might reveal to you your purpose? It has taken me submitting myself to doing His will in my life for me to get to the place were I could hear from Him. I would have hated to one day look back on my life to find I had no impact on this earth. I always used to think to myself growing up, "There has got to be more to me than this." Like the story of Esther, when her uncle Mordecai sent word to her saying, "... and who knoweth whether thou art come to the kingdom for such a time as this?" (Esther 4:14, KJV) Believe me when I tell you, "This is my time. I was placed here on this earth for such a time as this."

As a child of God, my assignment is to plant seeds of hope and encouragement into the lives of both the saved and the unsaved to give them a word from the Lord. Yes, I said the saved and the unsaved alike. Even we saved people have life issues and situations that we have to deal with. There are times when even our faith is tested. Giving your life to Christ does not mean that you will go without trials and tribulation. They will most definitely come, and if anyone tells you differently, they are not speaking God's word. "These things I have spoken unto you, that in me ye might have peace. In the world ye shall have tribulation: but be of good cheer; I have overcome the world." (John 16:33, KJV) No matter what you go through in life God has an answer if you turn your life over to Him. He is a forgiving God, so when we ask Him to forgive us of our sins and to come into our lives He does just that. He forgives our sins and never remembers them again. Is there anyone here on earth you can say that about? Remember, He is just one prayer away. Open your heart and mind to receive His word today.

WHO AM I?

Who am I? This is the question I have longed to find an answer to allowing me to be the woman that I am meant to be. I asked myself, "What makes me the woman I am?" Today, I realized that I am not just one woman, but also a combination of so many different women.

She's the little girl growing up feeling out of place in a home where she was constantly reminded that she just didn't quite fit in. She is a little girl growing from a child into a teen, constantly in a state of depression. She is the little girl who wonders if the horrible images of her childhood are real or just in her head. She longs for the answers to a hidden past; answers that never seem to fully surface. Scared of the past and the answers they hold, she engrosses herself in romance novels to create some symbolism of a real life without the nightmares. She becomes a teen wanting to know what it feels like to be loved because all she has ever known is being afraid and alone. Begging to be helped and feeling like a child again, she stays locked up in a room trying to be as normal as she possibly can.

She's the teen turned woman who marries the first man that asks her. She's so afraid because she's not beautiful enough; this could be her only chance, and if she missed it, she would spend the rest of her life alone.

She's the wife in hell praying every day to get out. She is praying for release but afraid to admit that she failed at the one thing she always knew she would be good at. So she stays.

After so many years of being called out of her name, being ignored, being lied to and cheated on, none of these things hurt as much as being used. When her body is used time and time again for another man's pleasures, she can do nothing about it. She could scream, but the children will hear. She could fight harder, but it will only hurt more. Once it's over, she just lies there. Once again, she's that child balled up in a corner not understanding what she ever did to deserve so much pain.

Freedom! God answers her prayers, and she is free. She's the single mother struggling to do the best she can to make ends meet, giving solely of herself for others, never asking for anything in return. A woman so tired that she has days where she just doesn't want to live anymore. She experiences days where she can't feed her children or herself. She's a woman that has taken a boyfriend that lies and cheats. That same man comes back after the relationship has ended and takes advantage of her body. Once again, she's become that child again.

She is a woman that watches her brother slowly

dying and wonders if that will one day be her fate. To die at such an early age and never experience the greatest gift on earth: *love, true love.* What a horrible thought.

Then suddenly out of nowhere she becomes the woman I am today. A black woman that is strong and full of tenacity. With the help of God, I have the willingness to make it through the hard times and the bad times no matter what the cost. I have released the childish things of the past and am now walking into womanhood ready to seize opportunities and experience adventures. I am no longer afraid of childhood memories because I have closed the doors of the past and am now walking through new doors.

I still have those days where I even question God, but I always know that He has my answers in waiting. Man doesn't understand my need for God; it's not for them to understand. When it is all said and done there is only one thing to remember:

Who I am is a child of God. The question you should ask yourself is, "Who are you?"

You've made it past *Who Am I?* which, in short, details my life in a nutshell. I wrote *Who Am I?* one morning as I was getting ready for work. I was dating someone at the time and I really wanted him to know who I was. First, it was amazing to finally meet someone I cared enough about that I would want him to truly know all my life's struggles. Secondly, I still really didn't know myself who I was.

As I prepared for work, God asked me, "Who Are

You?" He continued to ask me that same question, but I kept telling myself, "I'm going to be late for work". Finally, I stopped getting dressed and grabbed a pad and pen and began to write. *Who Am I?* was birthed in a matter of minutes, literally. That's how awesome God works! When you are filled with His word, finding yourself becomes easy. After you realize He has done some wonderful things in your life—like giving you peace about your past—then it is so easy to look back on your trials long enough to let it out and let it go.

By the way, if you're wondering what this particular friend thought of the writing I can gladly tell you that he never had the opportunity to read it. I could never bring myself to give my friend a copy because I told God that I wanted the man that would one day be my husband to be the first man to read *Who Am I?* I could never bring myself to give it to him because it wasn't meant for him after all. I attempted to let him read it on several occasions, but something inside me never felt comfortable enough to hand it to him. I even went as far as addressing and posting an envelope to him, but it would never make it to the mailbox. What I thought would be something I would only share with the man that would one day be my husband is now being shared with many. God had a bigger plan for *Who Am I?* He is, and can do, so much more than we could even think or imagine.

Take a minute before you proceed to really think about all of the things you have gone through in your life that have molded you, good or bad, into the person you are today. Find a quiet spot were you are able to think and meditate.

Take the time to write your own "Who Am I?" You will be surprised to learn what you truly think about yourself. Look to your heart, not your mind, for the answers. Your heart is where the revelation beings and deceit will end. Your mind will have you writing what others think you should be. Brace yourself for the rude awakening that is about to occur once you finish your own *Who Am I?* Don't cheat and don't fluff. Be open and honest with yourself. Remember this is the beginning of your healing process. Healing begins first with the truth. "And ye shall know the truth, and the truth shall make you free." (John 8:32, KJV)

Let's begin!

Despair

-To lose all hope or confidence; utter loss of hope; a cause of hopelessness[1]

Emotion

A state of feeling; a conscious mental reaction (as anger or fear) subjectively experienced as strong feelings usually directed toward a specific object and typically accompanied by physiological and behavioral changes in the body.[2]

And our hope of you is stedfast, knowing, that as ye are partakers of the sufferings, so shall ye be also of the consolation. For we would not, brethren, have you ignorant of our trouble which came to us in Asia, that we were pressed out of measure, above strength, insomuch that we despaired even in life:

But we had the sentence of death in ourselves, that we should not trust in ourselves, but in God which raiseth the dead: Who delivered us from so great a death, and doth deliver: in whom we trust that he will yet deliver us.

(II CORINTHIANS 1:7–10, KJV)

FRANCES A. OUTLAW

Deliverance

-the act of delivering someone or something: the state of being delivered;[3]

Life

The quality that distinguishes a vital and functional being from a dead body; the sequence of physical and mental experiences that make up the existence of an individual; one or more aspects of the process of living.[4]

The Spirit of the Lord GOD is upon me; because the LORD hath anointed me to preach good tidings unto the meek; he hath sent me to bind up the brokenhearted, to proclaim liberty to the captives, and the opening of the prison to them that are bound;

To proclaim the acceptable year of the LORD, and the day of vengeance of our God; to comfort all that mourn;

To appoint unto them that mourn in Zion, to give unto them beauty for ashes, the oil of joy for mourning, the garment of praise for the spirit of heaviness; that they might be called trees of righteousness, the planting of the LORD, that he might be glorified.

(ISAIAH 61:1–3, KJV)

Lost

Hopelessly unattainable; obscured or overlooked during a process or activity; not appreciated or understood[1]

LOST

How can one be Lost? Lost is a feeling so tossed and driven in my head. Lost is a lonely haven for me. Unsure of myself and of life. How do I move daily? Do I glide through the day? Do I stand still while the rest of the world passes me by? Why can't I catch up? Can't I feel the earth moving without me? Do I even see the people?

I see happiness in the people around me. In me I see nothing. I see a lost soul searching to be let free. I see a lost soul hungry for a chance to be loved. I keep searching, but I search in the wrong places. The places I search are dark and lonely. The hearts of those who I think love me are cold and empty. They don't love; they just use. They use the goodness in me. They use the love that I give them. Then they put me back into that lost dark place again as they move on with their lives to be free to love someone else. I am lost again, and this time I have fallen deeper into that dark place.

Lost is the love that's no more, and I don't know why. Lost is my mind because he won't tell me why. Lost is my heart broken and beaten. Lost is my soul because he has disconnected his from mine. We were once one, and he cut his away and left me for another. He left me to be lost and once again unsure of life and love.

Lost is not knowing how to fight anymore. Lost is not knowing how to win anymore. Lost is when giving up is all that you want to do. Lost leaves you broken. Broken and unable to pick-up the pieces. I see them lying at my feet. I see my heart there. I see my mind there. I even see bits and pieces of my soul there, but lost is all I feel. I know I should pick up the pieces, but why? Someone will come along and only throw them back at my feet again. Why keep losing myself to others. Maybe I should just leave the pieces at my feet and never let anyone near them again. Maybe at my feet is where they should stay. Better to be already lost than to start the lost all over again. It only took one thing to make me feel lost and broken.

Then, in the still of the night, someone whispered that He loved me. He wrapped me in the cradle of His arms. He poured out love and words of comfort. He gathered me into his bosom and He wiped my tears away. He led me to a place of peace where all my broken pieces were joined back together again. He handed them to me and said, "Broken you have come but whole you shall forever remain." Remember that His word says, *"For the Son of man is come to save that which was Lost"*.[2]

Have you ever felt lost? Have you ever felt like there was nowhere to go and no one to turn to? Well, the poem was appropriately named *Lost* because that is exactly how I felt while I was writing it. It's amazing going through something so many times and it not have an affect on you, but then, all of a sudden, that same type of situation will break you down to feeling like you are nothing.

"Lost" was written at one of the worst times in my life. It wasn't something that happened years ago but something much more recent. Although it's happened to me many times before, this situation took place during my walk with Christ. The inspirational writing of *Lost* came right after I found out that my ex-boyfriend had started dating someone else. Now, this should not have affected me, I thought. He was, after all, just another man that did not appreciate the love that I had to offer. No, this one was completely different. This one knocked me off my feet and I was completely unprepared for it. I was not prepared for the breakup, let alone the fact that I had to admit really loving him. Not that, "I love you just because your in my life at this moment," kind of love. Not that "I'm over him in one month," kind of love, but the kind of love that makes you want to stay in the bed with the covers over your head for a month! The bad thing about it was I was not supposed to be in love. I was not supposed to feel anything. I was the type of fighter who would never let an "ex" see me down.

I was that "smile-and-keep-walking-when-you-see-them" kind of person. Well, that girl never met a guy like him before.

In the days leading up to writing *Lost,* all I remember was being in a constant state of tears. I kept looking back on the relationship trying to remember what I could have possibly done to make him give up. For the first time in my life, with him I didn't think about the things that could go wrong. I just wanted to enjoy every moment. I found laughter, joy, and love all in that one relationship. I never thought that would be possible. I couldn't believe it was coming to an end. We were talking about building a life together. I could not figure out what happened. I believed that this relationship would weather any storm. Unfortunately, he didn't feel the same way.

When we met, life was good for us. I was going about my life having not really dated since I'd given my life to Christ. I thought that it would be easier to not date. I really was tired of the lies, the games, and the giving of myself getting nothing in return. So finally, I decided no more. I spent time alone—no relationships, no dating. I started taking time to get to know me, fixing the broken parts and learning to develop a stronger relationship with God. Then I met him. He was, I thought, an awesome man of God who was enjoying life, his relationship with God, and his work in the ministry at his church. There was an immediate attraction. Although I tried not to admit it, I fell for him the moment we met. I saw complete beauty in this one person. I remember thinking how beautiful he was. Not handsome, but beautiful. Handsome could not describe him. Beautiful was the only word that I could think of that did him justice. Eventually, I let my guard down and let him in. Believe me, I was definitely shocked that I decided to date him.

It's amazing. The very moment you think you've found happiness a problem develops. It never fails; when God starts blessing, the devil starts attacking. For once I was kind of glad that the attack wasn't focused directly at me but on him. It's taking me a long time to realize that the devil doesn't attack me when it comes to relationships or fighting for a chance at happiness. God has placed too much love, nurturing and commitment in me for him to attack me in that area. It takes a lot to make me want to give up. I have too much fight in me when it comes to the people I care about. The devil knew that was possibly a battle that he would not win; so, instead, he attacked him. He didn't attack the relationship outright, but he attacked all the other areas in his life. Immediately, our relationship suffered. It was a battle every day. We went from bliss to turmoil in a matter of weeks. I tried to do the only thing I knew to do and that was being there for him. I was available to talk when he needed me and tried not to push. It seemed the more I tried to help the more he pushed me away until he finally stopped speaking to me at all.

Now this is when Satan's attack on me started. When I did get to talk to him, I could get no answers. All I heard was silence and my guard was lifted again. I began to guard myself from what I knew would eventually come; so, I began to attack him with my temper to get him to talk to me. When we did come together to talk, I thought that we would try to work through our problems, but he had his mind made up, and there was nothing I could say that would change it. Finally, our relationship was over.

I was a complete mess! After a while, he moved on with his life and began dating someone else. While his life went back to normal when our relationship ended, my life was turned upside down. I went about my day working, cleaning, cooking, taking care of my children, and going to church all with a smile on my face. All the while I was feeling completely lost. How he could give up so easily? Why he couldn't, as a man of God, recognize the attack of the enemy trying to destroy our relationship? I couldn't understand why he wouldn't fight for us just as I was trying to.

For days I thought I'd gotten over it. One minute I was back to my old self and then the next minute I'd hear a song on the radio or one thought would cross my mind pushing me back to the same lost place again. My heart was crying and aching for the feeling to end. Walking down the halls at work, out of nowhere tears would stream down my face. I would have to make a mad dash to the restroom before anyone saw me. I would get home and not remember what I had done all day. All I remembered was the crying. All I knew was the horrible pains in my gut and chest, the swollen eyes and the need to sleep.

Finally, I was at a point were I just couldn't take it anymore. What was wrong with me that he didn't want me? What was so special about her that he could move on so quickly and try to make it work but he couldn't try with me? Why did all of his problems dissipate when he moved on? Instead of doing what I used to do throughout my life—locking myself in my room and not coming out, or spending days in bed trying to figure out what was wrong with me—I did something different. This time I was going to fight back. I was not going to let this beat me. I knew that I had something that was much stronger than my problems. I'd always known I had this option, but I never knew how to truly call on Him. This time, I had God on my side!

I had gotten to a place where I knew that I had no one else to depend on but Him. I didn't feel like I had anyone in my cheering corner rooting for me. Don't get me wrong, I had plenty of friends standing by my side to help me get through it, but I still felt that I was alone in a wilderness with no way of finding my way out. I knew if I ever wanted to smile again, if I ever wanted to be able to love again or let go of the hurt, then God was the only one I could turn to for the answers.

I got out of bed one morning feeling nothing. I didn't want to read my bible and I definitely did not want to pray. I was already one of those, "I'll only pray when I feel like it," kind of Christians. I didn't think that I was doing it properly anyway and my prayers would not be effective, so why pray? I thought prayer was something that only made since to do at night right before you go to bed. Praying during the early morning and all through the day did not seem right to me. This mentality, I realized much later, was the religion in me and not the Christian in me. There is a big difference. I decided that morning to give prayer a try even though I really didn't think that it would do me any good. Slowly, I began to pray not really knowing what to pray or how to pray. I remembered other Christians saying that praying to God was just like having a conversation with a friend. So, I began to talk to God like He was one of my friends. They were so right!

Praying to God is truly just a conversation between friends. God is that friend that knows all of your secrets and loves you in spite of them all. He's that true friend that you never have to worry about repeating those secrets to anyone. He is the friend you feel safe enough with that you let down your guard. I began to pour out my soul to Him. I started to explain my hurt and my pain. All the things He already knew. I begin to cry out to Him to help me get through this devastating time in my life where there were no answers and only more questions. Before I knew it I was engulfed with emotion. I felt God's presence upon me and I began to speak in tongues. As I continued to pray I could feel the heaviness being lifted off of me. Don't misunderstand, the feelings were still there, but the heaviness was gone. There was such a release! I knew then that He would take care of me and that my emotions were not too big for God. The disappointment was not too big for God to keep me as I went through them. It was then that I realized the awesome power of prayer. Prayer doesn't have a time. Prayer does not have a script. Prayer only has what you put into it and what you allow God to put in you.

After I finished my prayer that day, I sat on my bed when suddenly I found myself needing to write. I immediately grabbed my prayer journal with pen in hand not having a clue what to write. All of the sudden the word "lost" came to mind. Instantly, the words came but this time it was not a prayer. *Lost* was a written description of me.

Once I was finished, I jumped up off the bed and headed for the computer. I typed out the words from my journal and as I typed, the words seemed to jump off the page at me. I started really looking at what I had written. I didn't realize that this was an emotion and that it could be described. Most people describe their emotions by using words such as happy, sad, mad, and angry, but I was lost. I looked at the typed page and I could not believe those words came from me. I didn't think I had it in me, but what I've learned is that everything you'll ever need was placed in you before you were even born. I was never in a position to be able to release what God had placed in me because I was to busy feeling sorry for myself. I was to busy hiding away in my own little world; to busy pretending that my life was okay. Then, after I gave my life to Christ, I became busy learning how to be saved, developing my spirituality. I was so busy that I never sat still long enough for God to speak *to* me, let alone speak *through* me. Get the picture?

I remember just a couple of years ago I was renting a house. I had finally gotten to the point where I really wanted a home of my own, but I knew that my finances were really messed up. I was constantly worried about how I was ever going to buy a house. My girlfriend Pat called me and said, "Lisa, God wanted me to tell you that you will get the house and He will straighten out your finances so don't worry about it. He also said that He is trying to speak to you but you will not sit still long enough for Him to speak to you." I thought to myself, "What is she talking about? How am I not sitting still?"

I kept thinking I was staying in the word and trying

to be obedient to the things of God. I couldn't understand what Pat meant. It took me losing one of the most important people in my life to get me to a place of total brokenness in order for me to develop a stronger relationship with God. I learned to read His word and pray continuously, not just at night. I learned to just sit still and meditate on Him. It's during those times of meditation that He spoke to me the most. That's what she was talking about. When you forget your problems and just worship Him, this creates an opportunity for Him to speak to you and give you answers. But you have to know His word. For every problem that you have, God has an answer and His answers are in His Word.

In the mist of me learning to lean and trust in Him daily, not only did I heal from feeling lost but He also blessed me with the house and the finances, just like He said He would. Look back at your relationship with God. Have you made Him your friend? Are you talking to your Friend daily? Are you getting to know Him more each day by reading His Word? Do you know His Word? Have you learned to pray to God for yourself? Remember that your pastor will not be there for you always. If you believe God hears your prayers, then why can't you believe that He can also answer them? "And all things, whatsoever ye shall ask in prayer, believing, ye shall receive." (Matthew 21:22, KJV)

Loneliness (lonely)

Being without company; not frequented by human beings; producing a feeling of bleakness or desolation[1]

LONELINESS

Searching for someone to share my troubles with. Looking for another as lonely as I. Seeking but unable to find him. Is he hidden from my eyes? Why do I continue to search knowing that loneliness is all that will find me?

There is no joy in my loneliness. There is no pure smile in my loneliness. There is only loneliness to share my secrets with. Loneliness kisses my cheek when I'm alone, but there is no joy in its kiss. Loneliness hugs me when I'm afraid, but there is no comfort in its hugs. Loneliness says, "I love you," when I feel unloved, but emptiness is all I feel when it speaks.

What an empty feeling to have. What a sad feeling to endure. There is no one that loves me. There is no one to talk to me when loneliness comes to visit me. There is no one to share a part of me with. Loneliness is there, but it offers nothing. It gives me nothing. No words of wisdom. No words of comfort. It only offers itself. Loneliness doesn't care enough, but it's willing to stay around. There is no one to fight for me but loneliness. It wants me all to itself. There is no one bold enough to forsake what others say and proclaim, "I love her anyway," but loneliness will.

I did not know where this loneliness came from; it appeared suddenly one day. I did not seek it out. I did not search for it. Somewhere over the years of disappointment it keeps finding me. I keep asking it, "Am I not beautiful enough? Am I not smart enough? My hair does not flow down my back, but my love flows through every part of me." I may not be as beautiful on the outside as most, but God has given me a beauty inside that is more beautiful than that which is on the outside. I hold my head up high so that others will not see loneliness walking beside me. I fight a smile everyday so that loneliness will not show itself.

I struggle daily with uncertainties. I wonder if life just loves seeing me struggle and fight. I wake each day with loneliness beside me. I glide through the day with loneliness whispering in my ear reminding me that I am alone. When I lay my head down at night, loneliness is that stillness in the dark that will not allow me to sleep.

Why won't loneliness leave me alone? Why won't he leave me like so many others have done? I was searching for someone but loneliness is not he. I was seeking someone but loneliness is not what I seek.

On the loneliest of days I stumbled upon a door and decided to knock. Unsure of who would answer, I felt something inside. Then to my surprise someone opened the door. Not sure if it was fear or peace I entered anyway. The tears begin to flow. My heart began to pound. The uncertainty was answered as peace swept through me. He hugged me like loneliness did, but I felt comfort. He kissed me on my cheek like loneliness did but there was no more fear. He whispered to me in the dark, and I fell into a sound sleep. He walked with me and kept reminding me that he loved me. The smiles appeared, and my old friend, loneliness, forever disappeared. The tears became tears of joy. He did not have to stand in front of others to declare his love, because he declared it to me. He reminded me that when I did not know what to do I could just stand on his Word. He said, *"Ask, and it shall be given you; seek and ye shall find; knock, and it shall be opened unto you: For every one that asketh receiveth: and he that seeketh findeth; and to him that knocketh it shall be opened."*[2]

Looking back on the many times that loneliness has crept up on me, I've tried to pinpoint when it all begin. As hard as it is to admit, I must be honest, it's always been a part of my life. It's part of what has defined me over the years. I can't remember a time when loneliness had not attached itself to me; whether it was feeling out of place in my own home growing up, not having any real friends that I trusted completely, or in my relationships. Throughout the very few relationships that I've had, I always felt some form of loneliness—mentally or physically. Something has always been missing. Even during my nine years of marriage I can't remember a time that I didn't feel lonely.

Childhood

During my childhood—what little bit of it that I can remember—I was always trying to find somewhere I could be by myself; where I would not be bothered. My sisters used to tell me for years I was adopted because I was the only one of them that was different. I didn't like the same things that they liked. I couldn't dance or sing like they could. Even the ones that could not sing were artists. I remember that my brother had a collection of comic books that he drew of Spiderman and Bruce Lee. He painted pictures on the ceiling of his room. Even one of my sisters could draw beautifully, too. She would look at clothing in magazines, and if she didn't like an outfit, she would redesign it the way she thought it should look. All of them were dancers. They knew all the latest dances, but I, the black sheep of the family, could do none of those things. I couldn't sing. I couldn't draw. The only kind of dancing I liked was ballet and ballroom, not something you could admit proudly being from a black family in the country.

Teens

Early in my teenage years I realized that I had a passion for reading. I would spend most of my time engrossed in a romance novel to keep from having to deal with my family. I would close myself off in my room and start a novel and would not leave my room until it was finished. There were times that I would start a book in the morning and would be up until the early morning hours of the next day until I was finished reading it. My mother would have to make me come to the table to eat. There were many times when I would be the last one to the table and the first one to get up. My mother would make me put my book down and go outside to play just so that she knew that I was doing something other than reading. When my family would go to my relative's house I would stay home by myself as often as my mother would let me. I just didn't want to be bothered with people. I was better off by myself. I liked me and being alone; people on the other hand I wasn't so sure of. Don't get me wrong I loved my family; I just preferred not to be around them.

It wasn't until I became an adult that I realized that it wasn't that I liked being alone, but that I spent all of my childhood alone in a state of depression. I was alone because I chose to be alone based on the horrible images that would never seem to go away. I knew that something horrible had happened in my childhood and I figured that if I stayed to myself no one would figure out what it was. I was never going to be the person that destroyed our family. We were to close. We did everything together. Every holiday was a celebration; there was always some reason to get together. I was not going to destroy my family with my little secret. So I avoided them at all cost. It worked because no one suspected a thing. They all just figured that I was different. Can you imagine spending your entire childhood and teen years in a constant state of depression? I was scared to get close to anyone. Hating my life and wishing that I could have another, better one, I lived my life in a fantasy world of romance novels and television. I imagined my life being better than any of the characters in the books that I read or the shows I watched. Nevertheless, I always dreamed of having someone I could talk to and tell my secrets, so that I would no longer feel alone or rejected by the people that I loved more than anything in the world.

Marriage

If my childhood and teenage years weren't enough for you to understand my loneliness, then let's talk about the married years. Among other reasons, I decided to marry to escape the pains of loneliness. One of the biggest mistakes a person can make. There are those who eventually grown to love their mate, but then there are others whose relationships end badly or developed into a resentful, bitter union for many years. Marriage is a sacred union between a man and a woman before the eyes of God. Do not take this commitment lightly. Marriage is easier to get into than to get out of. Marriage does not cure the pains of loneliness.

I chose to marry someone that I did not love because we had a child together. I wanted to ensure that my child would not grow up without his father. I also believed because I was not beautiful and slim like the models on TV or other women I saw around, if I didn't take this chance at marriage it would never come around again. Boy, what a mistake! When it finally came time for me to get married, I was horrified. I realized then that I did not want to marry him and that I would regret it for the rest of my life. I spent days trying to figure out how to get out of it. I prayed that he would change his mind, joining me in deciding that this was not meant to be, and that we should just cancel the whole thing. It was no big deal since we were only going to get married at a chapel by ourselves. As much as I wanted to get out of getting married, I had to go through with it because I promised him that I would and I believed in keeping my promises. That should have been the one promise that I broke.

I spent almost nine years praying everyday to get out of it. Everyday I felt alone and that I had made the biggest mistake of my life. There was no love or affection throughout our marriage. We spent little to no time together. It was a marriage without laughter, without love, and without friendship. There were days when I would hate to see him come home from work. I used to think that one day the love would come, but it never did. The longer I stayed the more I disliked him. The more I disliked him the more I wanted to disappear.

Early in our marriage I realized that we had nothing in common. For example, we did not have the same values about family and friendship. He believed that if someone did you wrong then you get back at them and never let it go. I believed that you forgive them and move on. Furthermore, he did not believe in taking care of his family financially; so, I had to do it. This led to years of resentment towards him because he left everything up to me. I did not want to be the head of the household. I wanted a man that was strong and bold enough to take charge.

About two years into my marriage, I got to the point that I could not stand for him to even touch me. Having grown up watching my parents, I developed the belief that you were never to become intimate with anyone that you had no feelings towards. It was simply not something that you did. If there was no love there then it was just something that was not done. Sure, that is all fine and dandy unless you are married. How do you muster up the strength to become intimate with someone you don't love? How do you become intimate with someone that you don't even like? It was the hardest thing that I have ever had to do. The thought of it would make me cry. The minute it would begin, the tears would start streaming down my face. After it was all over, I would just ball up in a knot and cry until I knew I had to get up to get the children or until I cried myself to sleep.

I must admit that I spent six of the almost nine years of marriage completely dead inside with no desire for anything physical. At one point I thought that there was something wrong with me because there was no desire at all. This should not happen to a married woman. Well, let me enlighten you all. Marrying someone just because you think it's for the best, because your friends think you should, or because you have a child together is probably the worst thing that you could do to yourself and to the person that you are marrying. Don't cheat yourself or that other person out of waiting for the mate that God has for you both. It's not only your life that you must think about, but also that other person.

Loneliness comes to find even those who are married if the relationship is not right. I used to ask God what was wrong with me. Why was there no desire for my husband or was it I just did not have any desire for men at all? Finally, I realized it wasn't that I did not have a desire for physical companionship; it was that I had no love for my husband. Nevertheless, I stood on my belief that when you gave yourself to someone it was because there were emotional ties to that person; I had my wifely duties to uphold.

I didn't know how in the world I was ever going to get out of it. I did not want to admit failing at the one thing I always wanted more than anything: to become a wife and mother. Admitting failure, to me, was not an option. I would sit and think of ways to end my life just to get out of it. Death to me was the only way out. I would lie on the bed many nights with pills on the nightstand or a knife in my hand trying to make the decision to end it all. Then my children's faces would flash in front of my eyes and I couldn't bring myself to leave them. I remember always praying, "God I know that you have got something better for me than this. You have a better husband for me than this. You have a better life for me than this." Thank God my mother made us go to church, placing the foundation of the Word of God that we could carry with us throughout our lives. It was those teachings keeping me safe those many years when I turned away from the church. "Train up a child in the way he should go: and when he is old, he will not depart from it." (Proverbs 22:6, KJV) Because I was lonely my entire marriage, I eventually got the courage to leave and start my life over again. Unfortunately, loneliness packed its bags and came with me.

Relationships

As a single mother, I often times felt alone. There were nights that I would lie in bed with tears running down my face wishing for someone to just love me. I always dated men who enjoyed spending time with me, but they never wanted to commit to a relationship. The commitment of a ready-made family was too much. The fact that I could not have any more children didn't help matters, either. It was out of the question. They wanted children of their own to raise. Imagine how your heart stops beating for those few seconds, taking in the rejecting words from someone you love and thought you would spend the rest of your life with: "We can no longer be together because I want a child of my own." What can you say to that? Especially, when you yourself would love to have another child but can't?

Wishing that you could be the one giving them what they wanted more than they wanted you, you can't hate them, but you still wish they would choose you. That is a different kind of loneliness. So, you hope for someone that will love you despite all of that. Well, guess what? I found that very person and His name is Jesus Christ. I dropped my guard and stopped making excuses as to why He couldn't have me completely and just let Him do what He wanted to do with me. I'll tell you that was the hardest decision I ever made; but it was also the best decision.

The first two years of my salvation were hard. I was developing my relationship with God but I was also still trying to hang on to some of my sins from the past. I didn't want to give up the relationships that I had already formed in my life. I wasn't ready to give up fornication and hanging out at the clubs. I loved dancing and I was not going to give it up that easily.

Fornication was my way of not feeling alone. If I felt alone I would just call my ex-boyfriend and he'd drive down to spend the weekend with me. I didn't think there was anything to wrong with that. Plenty of Christians were doing it, I thought. There was no way Christians could possibly be dating without some form of intimacy. Well, the more I was being taught the Word, the more I became committed to it and the more I realized that I was out of the will of God. When God's Word convicts you to do His will and keep His commandments then you will willingly give up your sinful ways. It wasn't until His word rested down in my spirit and I understood His word when it says,

> I beseech you therefore, brethren, by the mercies of God, that ye present your bodies a living sacrifice, holy, acceptable unto God, which is your reasonable service. And be not conformed to this world: but be ye transformed by the renewing of your mind, that ye may prove what is that good, acceptable, and perfect, will of God.
>
> (ROMANS 12:1–2, KJV)

I've been divorced for several years now. Even though loneliness has come and gone over the years, now there is a peace in my being alone. There is a joy in my being alone. I pray to God to send me a husband. The husband He has for me. I wait patiently for that day, but until then I just bask in the glory of having as much time as I need with my Lord and Savior. Although I have children to take care of, they are now at that age where they no longer need my attention every minute of the day. What will happen until the time my husband enters the picture? I'll spend my days developing myself in the Word of God and praying and speaking to Him. He has my undivided attention. He has all of my time now, and that is the way it will remain until I remarry.

> "There is difference also between a wife and a virgin. The unmarried woman careth for the things of the Lord, that she may be holy both in body and in spirit: but she that is married careth for the things of the world, how she may please her husband."
>
> (1 CORINTHIANS 7:34, KJV)

I have developed a love for my time alone with God. There are times when I think about being married again and I wonder if my husband will need too much of my attention and if he will interfere with my time with God. Prayerfully, the husband God sends me will also appreciate his time alone with God, as well. For it is this time that I cherish my undistracted time alone with God.

What about you? Are you willing to give up some things and some people for God to really manifest Himself in your life? Are you willing to forsake what others say about you or your past and say, "Nevertheless, I will serve the Lord at all times?" Are you sold out for Him? God does not always give you what you want, but He will always give you what you need. Will you trust that He will do what He says He will do? Do you need Him today? Make the decision to surrender your life to Him totally and watch Him show up and show out in your life. Where God dwells there is no loneliness.

Stolen (Steal)

To take the property of another wrongfully and especially as a habitual or regular practice; to come or go secretly, unobtrusively, gradually, or unexpectedly[1]

STOLEN

Young and so misguided, I was unsure of what had taken place. Did I imagine the things in my head, or were they just misplaced? Someone has stolen what was mine to give. Someone has stolen a life that will now have to fight to live. How could they take what was not given? How could they steal such a precious jewel? A diamond in the rough. A stone that was not supposed to be touched. No longer do I glow or shine, for my body is no longer mine. No longer am I an undiscovered jewel, for it has been stolen from its hidden place before its time.

Someone wanted something that was not theirs. Someone took what was not given. How does one justify such terror? Hidden in a place of fear. I look for someone that will hear. Hear my screams in the dark.

Hear my cries in the night. See the fear in my face. Can't you hear me crying out? Someone, anyone let me out! Why won't someone help me? Why doesn't someone rescue me?

I can't say a word because my words will only bring pain. Mother doesn't know, and I can't break her heart. Father doesn't know, and I can't be the reason that he looses his mind. In secret is where my fears and horrors dwell. In secret is where my heart swells.

As long as I am distant from others no one will figure me out. Don't share yourself with others. Live without. At arms length is where you keep them. Your guard of protection you raise.

Expect nothing from man. Man will lie and take what is not theirs. Man will steal and kill what is left of you. They will steal your joy and peace. They will kill your spirit and soul.

"Fight for your life!" someone said. But how do I fight? What is there to fight for? Fight for more pain? Fight for more lies? Fight for a disconnected soul and mind? How do you fight what you can't see? Hidden layers of dishonesty! They enter in bringing you joy. A path of destruction lingering behind. They smile and continue on. Looking for another prey to take in. How can anyone commit such a sin? Alone you are left asking why, as you wait patiently for your soul to die.

"Die! Die!" you keep saying to yourself. Why continue to be put on a shelf? What kind a life can you live? There is none of you to give. Lost and Loneliness are the feelings you can describe but what happens when God provides. He tells me who I am. He is my comforter and protector. Protecting me from all danger, hurt and harm. When fear appears I can now sound the alarm. He swiftly stands and holds out His arms. All of my peace is within His reach. He sits me in my secret place but this time there's mercy and grace. He comforts me as He always does then He opens up the heavens above. It's when the heavens begin to open and the winds begin to blow that He says to me, *"The thief cometh not, but for to steal, and to kill, and to destroy: I am come that they might have life and that they might have it more abundantly."*[2]

Do you have an imagination? If you do, put your imagination cap on for a minute and go with me on a trip down memory lane to a place I call *Stolen*. Imagine going about your childhood happy and carefree. Then, suddenly, out of nowhere someone you know and trust takes your childhood away. This person takes away your security, your trust, and possibly your future. Can you imagine the fear? Do you feel the hurt? Can you describe the unbelief? That's what happens when your life is snatched from your hands without your permission. Like driving to an unknown place with a map in hand, but all of the directions on the map are wrong. That is what happens when you're forced to take a wrong turn on the road called life. Instead of driving straight ahead you end up at an intersection where you can only go to the right or to the left. You're desperately searching for the path that will lead you back to the right road, but now you have a long journey to take before you can ever make it back to the avenue of normalcy again. Trying to make your way back, your travels will have you making turns as if you were in a maze. Suddenly, you become fearful you may never get back to the road that will lead you to the path towards your deliverance. Thankfully, there is a force within you telling you *never* quit. Just keep driving; at least you are still making turns.

Eventually, you reach an intersection named the teenage years. You're going about your life thinking that everything is okay, and then, out of nowhere, comes this image that hits you in the face. The image is distinctive and vivid. It's powerful and terrifying. You see it so clearly it is as if you are on the outside of the scene looking at someone else—hoping it's someone else. But sadly, it is you. You're lying in a bed. Someone much bigger and taller than your childhood frame is standing over you. You are completely afraid, but you lie still. You've been here several times before. Slowly, you turn towards the doorway and all you see is your brother standing there. A brother only a year older, but from this day forward he's a giant in your eyes. You lay silently as he says, "If you ever touch her again, I will tell." That is the day it ended. Your life has a chance to take a new turn with new directions, guiding you to that ever sought straight and narrow road—or so you think.

Instead you fight everyday to keep it together. Every time that image pops into your head you wonder if it really happened or was just a dream. How could it be a dream when you're awake every time you see the same picture? It's as if you are looking into a mirror trying to erase the face staring back at you. But as much as you try, the same reflection of you flashes before your eyes, never changing. Nevertheless, you keep driving.

You are now about 30 years old, going through a divorce, and don't even have a dime to your name, when, all of a sudden, you come to that fork in the road called adulthood. You've just started a new job, trying to raise four children alone and you live in government housing. You work almost sixty hours a week just to make ends meet, learning your job so you can get ahead. Your children hardly ever get to see you and you have already started dating someone else. You're on the verge of a nervous breakdown and you don't know what to do.

Finally, you realize that you need professional help. This time hiding won't work; working ridiculous hours to keep your mind off your life won't do it either. So, you begin seeing a therapist who begins to try and break down the barriers you've built around yourself. The dissecting begins: first with your marriage, and then with this newfound relationship. You both find yourself getting nowhere because you realize that there is something much deeper that started long before your marriage fell apart. So, she recommends that you see a psychologist. You're thinking to yourself, "This is stupid! What in the world can a psychologist possibly get out of me that a therapist couldn't?" Nevertheless, you're desperate. What could it hurt?

You arrive at your designated appointment and you enter into his office and have a seat beside his desk. He introduces himself and goes over the information your therapist has given him about you and your sessions together. Then he begins to question you and coaxing out the fear of the images in your head you've had since you were young. Tears swell up in your eyes as he says, "So, you've basically been depressed all of your life?" Rivers of tears begin to pour down your face when you realize that he was right. Immediately, it seems as if a million thoughts cross your mind. *If he has figured that out in less than fifteen minutes someone else will too. What else would he get out of you if you continue to come? Will he eventually get you to the point that you not only remember the day that it ended but also the day that it began?* That you just can't have. You leave his office with a bag of pills that will help you sleep and a useless slip of paper with your next scheduled appointment. That appointment reminder isn't worth the paper it was printed on because he will never see you again.

From that day forward you lock away those memories, like you've always done, talking your way into being okay, pretending like nothing is wrong and continuing to work until things get better. Besides, once you're finally financially stable you won't even think about the other problems. Money solves all problems, right? Wrong.

Horror strikes about a year later when you find out your brother is sick. What in the world do you do? You drop everything and run to his side. While you're there, you find out that not only is he sick, but he is dying. The doctors are only giving him six months to live. Devastated, you look at him lying in that bed as he tells you this news and you try to speak but you can't. You immediately think, *you're the only one that knows my secret. You can't die on me!* He looks up at you, and although you haven't said a word out loud he knows your heart and says, "I know Lisa. I know."

At that moment, you lose all hope for anything good in your life. The one person that you've always had a special bond with is about to leave you. Although you haven't seen him in years, it doesn't matter. You don't know what to do but be there for him. And being there for him you will do. For him you will do anything. You turn your life upside down to make sure that he has everything he needs until the day he dies.

It's during this time that you realize that you can no longer let this dream haunt you. You have to let it go. So you make up in your mind to no longer look at the negative of the situation, only the positive.

I know your thinking, *What in the world could be positive in this type of situation?* Well let me tell you the positives. First, I made it through it. It didn't kill me. Secondly, it didn't destroy me completely, either. There was still some of me left, and it was enough to make me want to continue to live, love, and move on. Thirdly, I never allowed what happened to make me so bitter or angry that it would cause me to do something stupid like turn to drugs, prostitution, or becoming an abuser of people.

It wasn't until I began writing this book that I finally understood why God never allowed me to remember the rest of what happened to me. Remember God knows me better than I know myself. I remember the scripture where it says,

"There hath no temptation taken you but such as is common to man: but God is faithful, who will not suffer you to be tempted above that ye are able; but will with the temptation also make a way to escape, that ye may be able to bear it."

(I CORINTHIANS 10:13, KJV)

God is saying to you and me that He will never put more on us than we can bear. He knew what I could and could not handle. He gave me just enough to hold on to for this time but not so much that it would destroy what He was trying to develop in and through me. He is an awesome God! I made a choice to not let what happened to me cause me to lose myself and my love and respect for others. I took my situation and used it to love people more, to be more conscious of their feeling rather than my own. Sometimes it was a little too much and it cost me later. But what I have lost is nothing compared to what I have gained by helping those that need it. I have a genuine love and affection for helping people. Thanks to my Father above, who planted the Fruit of the Spirit in me long before I even knew what it was. "But the fruit of the Spirit is love, joy, peace, longsuffering, gentleness, goodness, faith, meekness, temperance: against such there is no law." (Galatians 5:22–23, KJV)

Okay, we've finally found that straight road again and arrived back to the present. Did you enjoy the trip down memory lane with me? I hope that you received something out of this journey, for every trip that you take there should be a memory that leaves a mark in your heart. Did you find a memory today? I hope that you did.

Fighting

To contend in battle or physical combat; to strive to overcome a person by blows or weapons; to engage in boxing; to put forth a determined effort.

FIGHTING

I fight for my life. Constantly fighting to be. Fighting to exist and yet I don't know why. I look around, and no one seems to be fighting but me. I fight each day to smile. I fight each night the desire to have someone by my side. How long does the fight have to go on? I fight year after year with the same results. It seems as though the fight gets harder as time goes by. How can this be? I look at myself, and I see kindness. I look again, and I see unselfishness and yet the same qualities I see others see as weaknesses.

Fighting the need to fit in. Fighting the empty parts of me that says, "Just do it, girl. You know that you don't want to be alone anymore." Fighting the anger in my heart that says, "You need to pay them back for the wrong and the hurt that they have done to you." How do I avenge myself when there is no revenge in me? However, the love I have for others makes me want to fight for them and not against them. Even when they hurt me their happiness is all that I want. How do I prove to them that they are the ones that are lost and not me?

I fight the urge to hit. I fight the urge to hurt. I fight the urge to explode so instead I explode inside myself. My mind begins to wonder. Wondering at such a fast pace that even I can't contain the thought going on in my head. My heart aches so uncontrollably that I feel my insides tingling. I want to scream, but I don't know if even the words would come.

I fight for my dignity! I fight for my self-respect! I fight for my worth! I fight for myself! I begin to question even God. How could you have made me so full of kindness? How could you have made me so giving? How is it that I am strong when it comes to protecting others, and yet when it comes to me, weakness sets in? Something in me should hate. Something in me should want to do wrong. Others are doing it, and they seem to be living a wonderful life. Why is it that I am the one fighting to exist? Why am I fighting to be whole? Why am I the one that craves goodness?

So I enter the ring prepared to do battle. I take a swing to the right and try to take out Fear, but it keeps getting up. I take a jab at Hurt, but it throws one back at me. I even try a left hook at Heartbreak, but it hooks me instead. I am black and blue from the hits of life. Several rounds have come and gone and defeat seems inevitable. Just before the last round, right before I decided to throw in the towel, someone rings the bell. I take a seat in my corner and with my head hung low I sit and wait for another loss to be called.

Then out of nowhere someone who has been watching since the fight began enters the ring and looks me straight in the eyes. At first I was frightened, but then I looked closely and saw that it was God. I could see goodness in His eyes. Kindness and gentleness were there, too. He reminded me that because He dwells in me kindness and goodness dwells in me also. He tells me that I did not have to be ashamed of the love that I had for others, for He is love. He stretches out His hands and gives me something shiny. He proclaims,

> "Put on the whole armour of God, that ye may be able to stand against the wiles of the devil. For we wrestle not against flesh and blood, but against principalities, against powers, against the rulers of the darkness of this world, against spiritual wickedness in high places. Wherefore take unto you the whole armour of God, that ye may be able to withstand in the evil day, and having done all, to stand."[2]

So I dressed myself with His armor, and I stood on my feet and entered the center of the ring. I took my stance in preparation for battle, but Fear would not enter. Hurt threw in his towel; however, faithful Heartbreak would not quit. As I was about to retreat, God looked at me and said, "*Keep thy heart with all diligence; for out of it are the issues of life".[3]* So as Heartbreak took his swing, I raised my shield of faith over my heart and quenched him with the sword of the Spirit.

I've always hated for anything to get the best of me. I would rather not attempt it if I thought I couldn't defeat it. As a teen, I really didn't understand what it meant to fight; I just existed. When I became a wife and a mother, I began to understand the meaning of fighting and not giving up. I had children to think about and they were my responsibility. Although I had major issues growing up, I did have a good life despite the horrible memories. I wanted to ensure that my children's lives would be so much better than my own.

All the fights I had encountered before were the kind of fights children have on the playground during recess. But now I was about to enter into a fight where gloves have to be put on and a few rounds fought. I was about to fight for the grand prize, but I had to first face my toughest opponent ever, me. I was about to exchange blows with the way I thought, how I handled each situation, and what I thought people had done to me. My lack of self-esteem caused me to allow what happened in my life, to rule my life. I refused to take control of my own existence. I waited on approval from others to make decisions about my life so I wouldn't have to. It was always easier to settle and be content with whatever people gave me. I didn't believe I was worthy of anything else. I didn't deserve their respect, trust, or their love, so I took whatever I was handed. Now it was time to put on my gloves. It was time to say, "No more!" This bout was for the real prize of my self-esteem, self-respect, and taking control over my own life.

Round One: Divorce

Making the decision to finally give up on my marriage was where the fight really began. I was in for the fight of my life, and my divorce was the easy part. I'm glad to say that my divorce, although bitter, was not long and drawn out. When I made the decision to end my marriage, I didn't try to hold on to a bunch of materialistic things that would have us fighting for months. I remember my mother telling me weeks before my marriage ended that materialistic things I could obtain again, but I only had one life to live. It was on that very day I made up in my mind that it was okay to say, "I give up." I walked away from my marriage with almost nothing. The only thing I was determined to fight for until the end was primary custody of my children. For that, there was absolutely no negotiation.

I left the home that I shared with my husband to move into government housing, but I determined in my mind that I would not live there any longer than necessary. For those who need it, there is nothing wrong with government housing, and it was there for me when I needed it the most. For me, it was a temporary living arrangement, and I refused to have my children grow up thinking that government housing was a way of life. I wanted them to be proud of me. I also wanted to prove to them that hard work would pay off for those who really tried.

When I left my husband, I had just started a new job. I enjoyed the work that I was doing, so I set out to learn as much about it as possible. I found myself working sometimes sixty hours a week, and the extra money came in handy. The downside was I found myself never spending time with my children. My youngest son had gotten to the point where he would not even allow me to hug him. Can you image the hurt when your child does not want to show you any affection? Nevertheless, I was determined to get us out of government housing. It took me almost a year but I finally did it with the help of my boss who pushed me to finally make the move. Once I moved out, I stopped working as much as I could afford and began focusing on spending time with my children again. It wasn't long before my son began showing me affection. The time away from my children was worth the sacrifice to give them a better home. I was determined to fight for a better life for them. In the end, I realized that the house, the job, and the money would never be more important to me than that of my family. Yes, it was worth the sacrifice. Although, there were some precious moments in my children's lives I was not a part of, I wouldn't change a thing. I know I can never get that back, but I realize it was all for a purpose. The divorce itself was easy, but life after the divorce was definitely the true test.

Round Two: The Move

Long before my divorce was final, I began dating someone that I had met through work. We spent a great deal of time together as he helped me to get through my divorce. He helped me settle into my new life without my husband.

Our relationship lasted for over a year until I finally ended it abruptly. Although our relationship was over, it did not stop him from wanting us to get back together. Telling him numerous times I was not going to change my mind did not convince him, thus, began the late night phone calls and the early morning knocks on my door. He did any and every thing he could to get me to talk to him, hoping I would believe whatever lie he was going to tell next. The more I said no, the more he persisted.

To add to my frustration was my ex-husband. He was working overtime, determined to make my life a living hell. He added to the late night phone calls, as well as many nights of him passing by the window outside my house at night while I tried to sleep. Can you imagine trying to sleep with the fear that at anytime someone could walk pass your window? He, too, did any and every thing he could to make sure I suffered. Whether it was making me wait for my child support or not picking up the children when he was supposed to, he made sure I never had any free time of my own. Both used similar tactics to achieve the same goal— my unraveling.

I held on as long as possible until I couldn't deal with either one of them anymore. My ex-husband wanted me to be miserable and my ex-boyfriend didn't want to let go. The late night phone calls and knocks on the door, the constant fussing and fighting all became unbearable. Neither one of them seemed to be listening when I said that it was over.

Once, I met a great guy at a business conference I attended. I found myself really wanting to get to know him better. We would talk on the phone for hours. The more I talked to him, the more I respected him as a person and as a man. We enjoyed each other's company, and I hoped that things would eventually progress to something more. But, in the meantime, I was just enjoying getting to know him.

Unfortunately, it seemed the more I got to know him the more the two other men in my life wanted to make me unhappy. The thing about it was that they had no clue that he even existed. Finally, my sister Wanda told me that I needed to move somewhere else if I ever wanted a serious relationship with anyone. I realized that she was right. If I wanted to build on the relationship with my friend or with anyone, I could not bring this kind of drama into his life. I respected him too much for that. I did not want him to regret ever knowing me. I wanted to try, at least, to experience having a regular relationship.

Although, I did not move right away, I constantly thought about it. I was too afraid to move away from the issues I had become accustomed to, even if they were negative. It wasn't until my brother got really sick that I finally decided that it was time to move closer to home. I decided that Savannah, Georgia would be a perfect place to live. It was almost a halfway point between my parents and my ex-husband. I wanted to be close enough to home so I could make the drive whenever my mother or brother needed me, but I also wanted to be close enough so my children could visit there father whenever possible. We had stopped in Savannah several times on our trips back and forth from North Carolina visiting my parents, and I was sure that was where we needed to go. Savannah seemed like the perfect location, but God has a way of ordering your footsteps without you even realizing it. He had a different plan in mind for me. I tried for months sending out resumes, making phone calls, applying for jobs and looking for a place to live, but nothing would come through. I was getting frustrated and I didn't know what else to do. There was no way I was going to quit my job and move to another city where I knew absolutely no one without a place to live or a job to work at. Then, one day I remembered a girlfriend of mine lived in Augusta, Georgia and something kept telling me to call her and ask her for help. Being stubborn, as usual, I refused to call her because I didn't want to move to Augusta. That was not my original plan. I didn't even know anything about the city. I saw it on the map but that was the extent of my knowledge. About two weeks passed. I was so irritated I felt I was going to explode if I did not leave Florida immediately. So, I finally gave in and called her. I asked her if she knew of any place in Augusta were I could rent an apartment or house for a couple of months until I could get a job and find somewhere else to stay. She told me that she had just closed on her new home the day before and she was planning to rent out her old house. If I was interested, I could rent it for two months until she had finished getting it ready for a renter. I jumped at the offer and move to Augusta, Georgia a few weeks later. Everything just fell into place.

I was in Augusta one month before I started looking for a job. One day I picked up a newspaper, but all I saw was work through temporary services. I had never worked through one before, so I kept looking over it. Then finally I decided I would go fill out an application the next day.

They called me back the same day, asking if I could come in the next day for an interview. Of course I went. And before my initial interview with the temporary company was over, I had two interviews set up for jobs only available that day. I went to both. Two days later I received a call from the temporary service offering me a job for the company I had prayed to God I would get. Not only did I get the job I wanted, but I also found a house to rent the next month. Isn't God good? Can you believe that during this time I was taking credit for it all? Round two was all about having the courage to leave everything I knew, starting over with four children in tow. I realize now that I was walking in faith even then.

Round Three: My Salvation

There were so many times in the beginning of my walk with Christ that I felt that I would be better off going back into the world. It seemed as though I had less problems and was never alone. I thought that I could walk away from it all and throw in the towel, but I realized that my life was better now than ever before. Yes, I was alone, I couldn't hang out like I used to, but I was happier than before. I didn't need a reason to smile, I wasn't hurting as much, and finally, there was nothing I needed in the world for me to go back to. God was all I had; all I needed. But still, I spent more time fighting the desire for the things in the world than focusing on getting to know God. When I took one step forward, I'd end up getting knocked back two steps by someone or something reminding me of the things I used to enjoy when I was out in the world. I dwelt on things that I used to do, regretting not being able to do them anymore. I thought being saved meant I would never have a full life. As a Christian, there was nothing I could do and nowhere I could go that would allow me to enjoy life; therefore, I didn't want to give in totally to being a Christian. Christians, I thought, led a boring and dead life. What a wrong perception of Christian living I had. Thank God for steadfastness and perseverance! Today, I can tell you I have never had a more fulfilled life than I have had since I have totally surrendered my life to Christ. It was a daily fight with flesh and mind, but I did not quit. I kept right on struggling because I was determined to not go back. I couldn't remember one thing from my past that gave me any kind of joy or peace. All I could remember were things that were taken from me. Studying God's word helped me to realize that what He had for me would be so much better if I held fast to His word and stepped out on faith. I took the step and now doors are opening up in all areas of my life.

I know you are thinking, *Why is she writing about this stuff?* Well, many people write books telling you that you need to change and what God will do for you if you do change. But how many books have you read that tell you what the changes entail? They tell you to give up your old sinful ways, but they don't describe what those sinful ways are. So, I decided to describe them for you. These are some of the things that you will have to give up and change if you want to live a full life as a child of God. You will need to change the way you think about different situations in your life. There is no sugarcoated message in this book. Like my girlfriend Cheryl says, "It is what it is." While you are thinking about all the things—these are just some of mine, and every person is different—you may have more or less to deal with than I did, but remember what God says in his word,

> To appoint unto them that mourn in Zion, to give unto them beauty for ashes, the oil of joy for mourning, the garment of praise for the spirit of heaviness; that they might be called trees of righteousness, the planting of the Lord, that he might be glorified.
>
> (ISAIAH 61:3, KJV)

He will always give you something in return; so, do not think you are giving up something for nothing.

Round Four: My Mind

Trying to work on "self" is a hard round to fight without getting bruised pretty badly. I had to look at my life and make the decision to change. I had to want to fight for myself. Not for my children and not for anyone else. I had to fight for me. I had to want a better life for myself and in doing so I would make a better life for my children. I wanted to be proud of myself. The first punch was having to face the demons from my past. I was in for the battle of my life in this round! The round began when driving back from visiting my brother in the hospital. I was talking to one of my sisters when she brought up the subject of things that had occurred in our childhood. Discussing what had taken place, she proceeded to tell me that she wanted to tell my mother. Unbeknownst to her, I panicked. I didn't know what to do. It ate me up inside; then, I realized that it was nothing to be ashamed of because I never did anything wrong. I was living a life full of secrets and if I would have just told someone, I would have saved myself years of hurt, pain, and mistakes. I had wasted many years hiding in fear of the unknown. I had lost time with my family, friends, not to mention messing up relationships, all because of my unwillingness to confront what had happened to me. That night, finally coming to grips with the innocence I had been denying myself, I began to heal. Someone else knew about my pain, shared their own pain with me, and yet they loved me anyway. Soon, the images from my past stopped showing up as much. I can probably count on my hand the number of times I've thought about that whole situation after that night. Since then, I've had to re-evaluate my life and the things that I've allowed to take place. I knew that it was time for a change. If I wanted to live, I had to first heal and figure out who I was. Never before had I taken the time to say what I wanted or did not want. I had to start fighting the parts of me not living according to God's word. It was time to cut away the fleshly parts of my being that were keeping me from living a full life, stopping me from receiving my blessings from God. This led me to come out swinging into the next couple of rounds.

Round Five: Drinking

There were a few rounds that were easy to win and drinking was one of those rounds. Luckily, I was no longer a heavy drinker like I was as a teenager. When I turned eighteen and joined the military, my first duty assignment was overseas, where, at eighteen, it was legal to drink. I begin drinking and partying as soon as I arrived overseas. My friends and I would start drinking on Thursday after we got off duty and hang out at the club until early the next morning. I would get back to the barracks just in time for morning PT (physical training). I would have a hangover trying to do push-ups and sit-ups, praying that it would end soon so I could go to my room and get a nap before getting dressed for work. The rest of the day would be spent drinking cups of coffee just so I could function enough to get my work done; all the while watching the clock, so I could get off and party all weekend. I would drink from Friday afternoon until early Monday morning. Until I found out I was pregnant with my first child, drinking and partying was all that there was for me to do. Most people say that it took them a while to stop drinking, but for me it didn't. The moment I found out I was pregnant my mothering instincts must have kicked in, and I put the bottle down. I did have a relapse of judgment about three months into my pregnancy. Mad at my husband, who was my ex-boyfriend at the time, I found myself drinking a wine cooler and partying at the club. I remember being sick the next day, so, needless to say, I didn't drink during my pregnancy after that.

I didn't start drinking again until after my divorce, but only when I would go out with my friends. I started hanging out at the clubs and partying, trying to make up for the almost nine years of marriage, living with a man who wouldn't even take me out, let alone allow me to go out on my own. It didn't become a regular thing like when I was in the military, but I still did it frequently. After I got saved, I stopped drinking the heavy stuff and started drinking only wine. I thought that wine would be okay as long as I did not get drunk. I would buy a bottle of wine every couple of months. Because I wasn't doing it on a regular basis, I figured I was safe. Well, when things seemed like they weren't going right, the more I felt alone, and the more I would drink. I began buying wine on a regular basis. I would drink a glass of wine almost every night to help me sleep. It wasn't until about two months after I started drinking daily that I realized that this was becoming a pattern. I began to see images of my parents when they used to drink. Drinking was an all too familiar thing in my family, and I refused to repeat the cycle. I went into the refrigerator and grabbed the open bottle of wine along with the other one waiting to be opened, and I emptied them down the sink drain. I know that some people believe that although you are saved it is okay to take a drink every now and then; but, I made up in my mind I was not going to put anything in my body not pleasing to God and that included alcohol. I developed a new found love for sweet tea and soda. Round won.

Round Six: Partying

Partying, or what most people call "clubbing," was harder to give up than drinking because I loved to dance. Like I said in one of the previous chapters, growing up I did not know how to dance, so I was always being told that I was different because of this. Well, when I joined the military and started hanging out at the clubs, guys I met would teach my friends and I the new dances, and we would learn them right there on the club dance floor. If the club doors were open, I was there. Nothing stopped me from hanging out at the clubs until, like with drinking, I got pregnant and stopped going all together. Then I got married and my husband did not like me hanging out, so I didn't go (even though he went all the time). Once we divorced, I started going again. Every chance I got, I was going dancing. I tried to continue going even after I got saved. I was only going to dance not meet men or drink. I just had a passion for dancing. Then one night I went out by myself, which was unlike me to go somewhere alone. I walked around the room and all of a sudden I felt out of place. This had never happened to me before. I didn't even want to dance. After about an hour of being there, I stood off to the side of the dance floor, watching people as they danced. I felt disgusted. Abruptly, this feeling came over me. I had to get out of there. I remember thinking to myself, *You know you don't belong here anymore, don't you?* I turned and walked out of the club. I haven't been back since. I learned to dance glorifying God as I praise him in the comfort of my own home or at church during Praise and Worship. I didn't have to give up dancing; I've learned to dance to a different beat.

Rounds Seven: Cursing

I tried cursing when I was a teen, but I never really got the hang of it. Then I became a professional when I joined the military. There was hardly ever a conversation of mine that did not have me saying several curse words, unless, of course, I was around my mother. I might have been an adult, but I would never be old enough where it would be permissible for me to curse in front of my mother. Even in my thirties, I guarantee my mother would *still* beat my behind if I disrespected her in that way. Believe me when I tell you that Elaine (my mom) didn't then, and still does not play! My filthy mouth was awful! At one point I thought I would never get cursing under control. I'd done it so long that it was an automatic way of talking. It flowed out of my mouth as easily as saying "good morning" or "hello." My children grew up with me cursing. There were times I would get so mad at them that I would curse in front of them. To them, it was another form of speaking.

Even after I got saved, I still cursed. When I gave my life to Christ, I had to make a conscious decision to change and do better. All of my sins did not disappear the minute that I gave my life to Him. He forgave me of my sins, but I had to renew my mind about the things that I did and said. I set out to defeat this thing called cursing. So, I started saying confessions about the way I talked and the things coming out of my mouth. "Let no corrupt communication proceed out of your mouth, but that which is good to the use of edifying that it may minister grace unto the hearers (Ephesians 4:29, KJV). I began to watch what I was saying, and slowly I begin to see a change in the way I talked. Eventually others begin to notice the change, also.

The more I fought the desire to curse, the more I began to become more aware of others doing it. I found myself squirming when I would see a movie or pass someone on the street cursing; especially if I saw a woman doing it. One day, while I was in the store shopping, I heard a woman cursing and I thought to myself, *Did I use to sound like that? That is not attractive at all.* For the first time I felt ashamed of my cursing and conduct. This is one round I'm still fighting. There are times when I may slip, but I am determined to win this one. By the way, did I mention that I am not perfect? God is not through with me yet.

Round Eight: Temper

This round took me totally by surprise. If you let me tell it, I never really had a temper—or so I thought. Now, if you let others tell this story they would *definitely* disagree with me. Until two years ago I would never have admitted I had a temper. To this day I still wonder where it stemmed from. I was never intentionally mean or nasty to people. I tried to always treat everyone with the utmost respect, so I was surprised to hear people tell me that I a temper. I thought that they were all crazy. Me with a temper—Never!

Now, I'm willing to admit that I did indeed have a temper, and it was not pretty. When I was mad or scared, I would say whatever I felt and would think about the words later. It was like a volcano exploding. If I let anger build up from something someone did or said, I would finally get mad enough to speak my mind. The lava of words would spill over wherever they may, and before it was all over, people would think twice about making me mad again.

I never understood the consequences of letting things build up inside of me, instead of handling the situations whenever and wherever they took place. Then, one night at Bible Study, my Pastor taught a message he called "Building Up and Not Tearing Down." He dug in deep about the real meaning of the Bible verse in Round Seven (Ephesians 4:29) and the following verse 30. It not only means cursing, but it also includes how you talk to people. I remember him saying you can destroy someone with the words coming out of your mouth. During the whole service, I could not even lift my head up from my Bible because I was guilty of what he was speaking on. Just that week I had completely lost my temper with someone that I loved very much. I said some very mean and hateful things because I wanted him to hurt just as I was hurting. I not only felt bad about what I said to him, but, because for the first time it really hit home, I was displeasing God. I ran out of service that night and jumped in my car. Before I could even get out of the parking lot of the church, I began to cry uncontrollably. I drove down the road, asking God to forgive me for the way I conducted myself and for disappointing Him. I asked Him immediately to forgive me for my sin and for hurting someone else. I made a vow that night to change. The next morning I called the person I lashed out at and asked him for forgiveness.

I've had to learn to think first and get my temper under control before I speak. I've also had to learn to not speak at all when I'm angry, but to calm down first or walk away if need be. I've learned to not take what people do or say so seriously because I can't change people or the way they think. It is okay to be angry; I just have to remember that God says, "be angry and sin not." It feels good after all these years to not be angry anymore. It feels good to not be bitter and want to hurt or hit. I now look at situations and assess them for what they truly are. I laugh at my children sometimes because I believe they think that I have completely lost my mind when they know they are in trouble for something. They stand around with this wide-eyed look on their face waiting for me to blow my top while they tell me what they've done. But guess what? They're still waiting. This doesn't mean that I don't get angry or emotional sometimes, but developing and intimate relationship with God and having Pastors ministering to me continuously, whether I like what they say or not, has taught me how to actually live by God's words.

Round Nine: Fornication

Let's just say that I would rather have dived into a pool instead of giving this one up. That may not sound like much to you, but I have always been afraid of heights and water. The two together were definitely unthinkable. I can't remember a time in my adult life when I've ever been without a man. Even though I've always had the self-esteem issue, never thinking I was beautiful, I was always able to get a boyfriend if I wanted one. Even after I got my divorce, I couldn't remember going longer than four or five months without a man. The first boyfriend I had when I moved to Augusta told me one day that I held on to past relationships just in case things didn't go right with my present one. I told him that he was wrong, knowing deep down inside that he was right. But being right still did not make me want to change. Men were my security blanket for loneliness. Even though my relationship with them was platonic, I had the option to go back if I decided. So, I chose to not end the friendships.

Then one day, after another failed relationship, I got fed up with dating. I realized that I wanted something more than a casual relationship that would never lead to anything. I wanted to be married again; it was time for me to make some changes if I wanted to be ready when God blessed me with my husband. First, I had to finally let go of those past relationships. Slowly, I started pulling away from them all, but I still kept in contact with them every now and then. I thought that this was letting go. It wasn't until I fell in love that I begin to fight this round with power. One day, while having a conversation with my friend, my phone began to ring non-stop. I could see the look in his eyes as he tried to control his anger. I felt my heart sink just looking into his eyes. I never wanted to see that look again. After that night, I said, "No more." I began cutting off all contact with my old friends without hesitation. I realized that I may not have gone about it the best way, but I did it. We broke up right after that, but I took that opportunity to learn what God had to say about relationships, fornication, and what an unmarried woman should focus on. I began looking up as many scriptures as I could to find about all three, studying and applying all of them to my life. I wanted to make sure that if we ever had a chance to rebuild our relationship, there would be nothing standing in our way. If that never happened, God had someone already picked out for me; I just had to stay focused and committed to doing His will and let Him take care of the rest. I spend my time learning what it takes to be a wife and a helpmeet. I made God my husband, and he began to teach me the proper way to have a relationship and how to become that Proverbs 31 woman

I continually pray to one day be. Preparation is the key. Are you prepared?

Round Ten: Finances

My finances were as messed up as I was. I went day by day pretending that my financial problems did not exist. I was tired of fixing problems, even my own. I paid what I needed to survive, which was all I could really afford anyway, and I didn't worry about the rest. Then one day my sister Rhonda gave me a VHS tape of Juanita Bynum called *No More Sheets*, where she talks about being prepared for relationships. She talked about having something to bring to the relationship: a car, a house, some property or even a bank account. I looked around and the only thing I had that was mine was my car and, technically, that wasn't even mine because I was still making payments. What she said stayed with me.

I started asking questions about budgeting and getting out of debt. A co-worker of mine helped me set up a budget to begin paying off my debt. I went to financial seminars at local churches, and in doing so I learned God's word on finances. By the time I closed on my first home in Georgia I'd paid off eighty percent of my debt.

> Owe no man any thing, but to love on another: for he that loveth another hath fulfilled the law.
>
> (ROMANS 13:8, KJV)

The rich ruleth over the poor, and the borrower is servant to the lender.

(PROVERBS 22:7, KJV)

I endured ten rounds of fighting, each one a little harder than the next. There were times when I got tired of fighting; then, there were times that I wanted to throw in the towel, but I continued on. Whether I was black and blue at the end of the fight, or if I came out smelling like roses, I was determined to finish this struggle. Coming out of a brawl smelling like roses may sound good, but there was not one round where that actually happened. I was just glad that I managed to climb out of the ring at all. I didn't have to throw the right punches each time. I didn't have to connect with each blow that I tried to take. What I did do was make contact when it actually counted. I wish I could say that I won the fight, but I'm still fighting. There will continually be rounds to fight, but with a renewed mind and the determination to stay committed to God's word and his commandments, I'll become better trained at sticking and moving. Still, some rounds will be harder and then some easier to bear. Don't be surprised if throughout your life you find yourself faced with fighting the same rounds at some point because the devil always tries to remind you of your past. Regardless, your goal is to keep the whole armor of God on and guard yourself from the wiles of the enemy. God will always be there to give you water when your thirsty and to dry the tears from your eyes and bind up your wounds.

Struggle

To make strenuous or violent efforts in the face of difficulties or opposition; to proceed with difficulty or with great effort.[1]

STRUGGLE

A tug-of-war going on inside my head. Should I hold on or should I let go. Should I have the faith the size of a mustard seed, or should I cast my faith away and say what I always used to say, "God does not care!" So I struggle with my desires. I struggle with my wants. Should I want what I desire, or am I asking too much? What if my desires are not God's desires? How do I let go and move on?

I struggle with patience. For it seems as though waiting is all that I know to do. I struggle with trust because, in the end, there is never any truth. I struggle with hugs and kisses because they are the signs of deceit. I struggle to be heard. Struggle for someone to hear the song in my heart. Feel the love in my soul. See the joy of my spirit. I struggle to be seen for who I am.

I wish someone would see the goodness and the

love within me and be satisfied with just that. For I am someone wanting to be held. Someone just wanting to be loved. To be treated with dignity and respect. Striving to be a virtuous woman and yet still learning. Not wanting to have to pass anymore test. Please, God, I just need some rest. Rest for my weary soul. Rest for my wounded heart. Rest for my mind and spirit still searching to be whole.

My quest for no more days of struggle is never ending. For as long as I am a child of God, trials and tribulations will come. I wish that trials and tribulations would for once forget my name. They never seem to let up. They never seem to let go. They keep saying, "One more trial. Just one more tribulation and she will blow." So they throw their fiery darts and attack from all sides, but they keep forgetting that God resides. As the darts come and the flames roar high, I lift my head to His Majesty on high. He dispatches His angels, and they encamp all around me prepared to fight and douse the flames of struggle and shame. For trials and tribulations will come but I must remember that,

> "We glory in tribulations also: knowing that tribulation worketh patience and patience, experience, and experience hope: and hope maketh not ashamed; because the love of God is shed abroad in our hearts by the Holy Ghost which is given unto us. For when we were yet without strength, in due time Christ died for the ungodly."[2]

Insecurities and low self-esteem were the biggest issues I struggled with growing up. I never felt good enough, pretty enough, or smart enough. It was more important to me to fit in with the "in crowd" than to concern myself with my education. I made it a point to make sure I didn't seem as smart as my friends, especially in High School. Wanting my friends to think I was not really into school, I hardly ever did my homework. I remember once my English teacher asking the class to write a paper. A couple of days later, I was sitting in the back of the classroom waiting for her to hand out the graded papers when she stood up in front of the class and proceeded to tell us about this wonderful paper someone had written and how she was going to read it aloud. Barely paying her any attention, I continued to sit in my chair, watching the clock, waiting for class to be over when she began to recite the essay. Suddenly, I felt my heart sink, realizing it was my paper that she was reading! I felt myself getting sick. I could not believe that she was reading my paper. Several of my friends were in my English class, and all I could think about was that they would know that I was not as dumb as I pretended to be. I was getting a compliment from the English Teacher, the *Advance English* teacher at that. This was not happening. By the end of the class, I was completely embarrassed. After that day, I refused to write another paper in her class unless it was absolutely necessary. Now that I think about it, I don't know how I passed the class because I sure don't remember doing much of the required work assignments.

Years later, I sent for a copy of my High School transcript. When I opened it up, I looked at the grades.

Although they were not bad, I began to chastise myself because I knew, like I knew then, that I could have done much better if I would have not allowed peer pressure to distract me from doing what I was supposed to do. If I had taken the time to look around, I would have seen there were others in our group that were making good grades and were still accepted. I can't go back and change what I did wrong in the past, but I certainly can use the realization of the wrongs done then, to strengthen me now. Remembering mistakes of the past encourages me to do what I need to do currently, regardless of the people or the circumstances.

Struggling with low self-esteem, I failed to realize that it was okay to be smart and popular at the same time. It was okay to have a passion for reading, math and science. It was admirable to have a passion to want to succeed and want something better for myself. But the biggest realization was that it was okay to be me. I didn't see it back then, but I definitely see it now.

My writing describes the many areas of my life that I struggle with, and throughout this book I'm sure that you have seen the many examples. Being the imperfect person that I am, I still struggle with my faith sometimes even today. My latest struggle with faith was with writing this book and the knowledge that this was God's assignment for me. I questioned Him about my purpose. I had three poems I had written, but didn't know what to do with them. I wrote them, then filed them away, thinking they would be something I would look back on every now and then. I shared one with my mother; of course, she swore I could write cards for Hallmark! Mothers, what an awesome creation by God they are; they will make you feel like you are the Rockefeller of anything you want to do. But seriously, even when you know it's not deserved, who's not going to want to hear praise? So, wanting a little more of that motherly stroking, I called her to read her my second poem *Loneliness*. Unbeknownst to me, she had my sister Rhonda listening in on the other line. When I finished they both complemented my work, telling me all the things I could do with what I had written—cards, books, plays, you name it. There was a level of joy that came over me. I had people that loved me enough to think that I could accomplish what I myself could not even imagine possible. In my mind I couldn't imagine writing a card, much less a book. I told them people would think I was psychotic because one person should not have all these types of emotions. Although my writings were all based on emotions I had lived through, I knew also that they were words anointed by God. A couple of days later I began to think about that conversation. I asked God what was the purpose of the poems. While driving down the road, God gave me the title of this book *From Despair to Deliverance*. I knew then that He had answered me. I responded, "God, everybody's writing books. I'm not a writer. But if you say so, I'll do it." Submitting myself unto Him, keeping His commandments, and fulfilling what He has purposed for me to do is all that He asked.

> Cast not away therefore your confidence, which hath great recompence of reward. For ye have need of patience, that, after ye have

done the will of God, ye might receive the
promise.

(HEBREWS 10:35–36, KJV)

Even though I knew I was on an assignment from God,
there were times when I still questioned the purpose of this
book. I've questioned the revealing of my life, my fears,
my secrets and my mistakes, but each time I realized that,
regardless of my fear of what people would say and how
they would react, God's will would be done; for I no longer
focus on the thoughts of others towards me, but I dwell on
His thoughts of me. "For I know the thoughts that I think
towards you, saith the Lord, thoughts of peace, and not of
evil, to bring you to an expected end" (Jeremiah 29:11, KJV).
He placed me on an assignment to write this book and,
unlike when I was in High School, I am no longer concerned about peer pressure. This paper, too, will be read out
loud. I may not get an "A," but I won't fail because I didn't
complete the assignment.

Hurt

To inflict with physical pain; to do substantial or material harm to; to cause emotional pain or anguish to.[1]

HURT

urt is a feeling that only I can describe. It's how I feel when tears come to my eyes. Years of hurt have passed me by and it still keeps happening. I wonder why?

Out of nowhere he appears and he's not the picture of the man I had in my head, but he's the man of my dreams and the answer to my prayers. He finally convinces me to give him a chance. Immediately, we both begin to make plans. He tells me of the life that we will one day live, and we make a promise that this will never end. He tells me about all the things he has to do, but me he never seems to include. He speaks of all his family and friends, but I never get to say, "How do you do?" He can't take the chance; his family would be appalled. What would they think? My life sounds so hard. Let's not forget that they haven't even met me yet. Just face it girl, you didn't pass the test.

Then one day, out of the blue, he comes to me and says, "We're through." Not even one reason why just that it was time to say goodbye. Then I realize he's kept me in his hiding place for only him to enjoy, and suddenly I remember that no one ever knocked at the door. He says that it's him and not me and at least on that one point we can agree. He's not concerned about his feeling or mine. He's more concerned about keeping his image alive.

For him it is no longer about his joy. He cares more about what's in store. The people he must impress and his position in life. Fortunately for me, people were never an issue. I only cared about my mission. I didn't care about what people thought or if they were impressed. I just wanted our union to be blessed. He tries to forget about the gift of laughter that we shared. He wants to forget the gleam in his eyes whenever I pass by, trying not to remember the love that he must let die. He must keep this undercover. No one must discover that it's me that he desires. So what else is there for him to do? He must forsake his love, walk away and be tough, for God's blessing of me was not enough.

He has moved on to another. The picture image he was trying to discover. He takes her out and shows her off. He dances and prances her in front of my face, and I say to myself, "Why not me? I have grace." He finally has what he's been wishing for, but I keep asking myself, "Shouldn't he want more?"

I spent months trying to understand what it was about me that he thought was inadequate. Was it because I was a single mother of four or the fact that I could not have more? Was it my desire to be faithful to the things of God? Was it my commitment to God's word and my total surrender to do his will? I have slipped and fallen several times over the years, but I finally said, "On these issues I must deal." No longer can I compromise and no longer can I hide, for God has given me a purpose. With this purpose there can be no disguise. Come clean with all your issues, for healing must take place. For this is just the beginning and you must finish this race! *"Know ye not that they which run in a race run all, but one receiveth the prize? So run, that ye may obtain."²* So I take the hurt and I take the pain for no matter what, God will sustain. For He says in His word, *"For his anger endureth but a moment; in his favour is life: weeping may endure for a night, but joy cometh in the morning."³*

When you've been hurt by someone you love it is a devastating feeling not easily recovered from. Hurt feelings caused by someone saying something that bothers me, I can handle. Being hurt because I didn't get a position that I wanted, I can handle. And, of course, receiving a cut or a bruise is nothing to a tomboy at heart. Someone I care about hurting me might take me a while to get over, but being hurt by someone that I love requires a longer process of healing, taking more out of me than I care to admit.

Losing someone that you love, truly love, is almost like

being stabbed in the heart. You feel an aching in your heart that never seems to go away. There's a tightening in your chest whenever you dwell on the hurt. No longer do you have an appetite for food. Crying seems to be a daily routine. Having fun seems to be useless because your mind is still focusing on the hurt that you've just endured.

I spent hours, days, weeks even months trying to figure out what happened to cause me to lose the person I loved. Looking for answers only left me with more questions than before. I began to blame myself for what happened. I could not figure out what was wrong with me. Why didn't he want me? An age-old question of a breakup that is not mutual. Then I realized it wasn't me with the problem. There was nothing wrong with me. I had to realize it was the other person. He had his own reasons for walking away, and maybe, just maybe, he had his own issues that had nothing to do with me.

Looking back on the relationship, I may have not done everything right, but I gave the relationship my all, which, for me, is saying a lot. I stepped into this relationship for the first time without reservations; therefore, I didn't put on my armor to guard my heart like I was supposed too. I didn't worry about the fact that he was a man, forgetting my belief that all men did nothing but lie. I didn't worry about this one breaking my heart because I knew from day one that this one would be for keeps. I made the mistake of just living in everyday of the relationship. I gave all that I could, but it was not enough. He still walked away. He had his own reasons and I had to except it, but it doesn't mean that it didn't hurt. There was nothing else to do but get over the hurt and move on. Yeah, right! Just how exactly do you do that?

I don't know about you, but I have learned to use the word of God for every situation that I've had to endure. It was the word of God that kept me going. I began to pray to God for answers, for healing and for peace about the situation. It took time, but He gave me what I asked of Him. There were several times that I broke down during prayer like a weeping child, crying uncontrollably. I went to Him in total brokenness because He was the only one I trusted with my hurt and pain. It was Him that comforted me. He saw the hurt that I didn't want others to see. I went into my secret place of prayer where He met me with open arms. He didn't say, "get over it girl." He didn't laugh at me and tell me that I was stupid for falling in love. He didn't talk about me behind my back. He didn't make excuses about what was wrong with the other person to get me to see the bad in him. He did none of that. What He did do is get me to a place of calmness, through His word, so He could speak to me. It was during this time that I began to truly develop my passion for the things of God. It was through my brokenness that He began to use me. He got me to a place where I was willing to let Him heal the destruction in my life. I'm not talking about the damage of the relationship alone; He had to fix all injures from my past that were still buried in the graveyard of my soul. The breakup was just the catalyst that was used to get me to this point. He had to get through those dark places in my past that I refused to let go of. It was time to dig those graves back up and confront them all.

The many feelings of despair in this book are

representations of the crypts that were uncovered from the burial ground of my past. The chapters are a description of the many emotions that I masked, never wanting to see again. If I didn't see it, I didn't have to confront it. While writing this book, I came to the realization that what I refused to confront was causing me to not live a full life. As I would write the chapters, they began to get harder and harder for me to complete. I began to have a flood of emotions that I didn't know what to do with. There were several times that I felt completely torn trying to write. My emotions were so uncontrollable I was scared for God to give me the words because I was knew of the emotions that would come with them. As fearful as I was about the next writing, I refused to quit because I knew that my assignment was much bigger than my emotions and fear. I knew that no matter what, I had to get over my emotions and keep on going. In doing so, I found myself healing from the pain I wrote so vividly about. I found myself reading each chapter over and over again, eventually incorporating the feelings and the scriptures referenced in the writings into my prayer. I became a stronger prayer warrior.

God not only healed my hurt from a broken relationship, but He healed the broken-down parts of my past. He had to heal these parts of me in order for me to get to the place He has me in right now—deliverance.

> The Lord is nigh unto them that are of a broken heart; and saveth such as be of a contrite spirit. Many are the afflictions of the righteous: but the Lord delivereth him out of them all. He keepeth all his bones:

not one of them is broken. Evil shall slay the wicked: and they that hate the righteous shall be desolate. The Lord redeemeth the soul of his servants: and none of them that trust in him shall be desolate.

(PSALMS 34: 18–22, KJV)

He filled my life with beauty instead of ashes, joy instead of mourning, and gave me the garment of praise as a replacement for the spirit of heaviness. How is your life today? Do you see ashes? Are you in mourning? Is your spirit heavy? If you answered *yes* to any of these questions, can I suggest to you one solution to them all? Try Jesus! I can't promise you that the road will be as easy as the song says, but I can promise you that your life will never be the same. We are always so willing to have faith and trust in men we can visually see, only to find out man can only do so much. How about trying a man that you can't see? Try the man that knows the number of hairs on your head—the one that knew you while you were yet still in your mother's womb. He is the one that remembers every tear that you've cried. He's the one that was with you every night you lay awake asking Him why. Let Him be your Comforter today. Allow Him to minister to your spirit and take the hurt away. Are you willing to surrender all to Him? Place all of your cares on Him for He cares for you. I'm not asking you to leap. All that I'm asking is that you take one step.

Scared

Thrown into or being in a state of fear, fright, or panic.[1]

SCARED

What is scared? Scared is possibly being alone forever. Not knowing real love ever. No real friends of your own. Scared is dying alone and never being missed. Scared is flashes of the same image that you can't figure out. Scared is not feeling safe in your own home so you sleep on the floor beside your bed. Scared is not even feeling safe on the floor beside the bed so you move to the cold and lonely bathroom floor. Doors closed, phone in hand, and you are in the fetal position, hoping and praying that the feeling of being scared will be overtaken by sleep.

Scared is a beating heart against your chest. Pounding so loud that you can hear the sounds. Sweat pouring down your face. Hands shaking, knees knocking, and then a sudden feeling of weakness hitting your legs. Your mind loses all thought. Life flashes before your eyes. All you can see is that moment. All you care about is what happens next. Hoping someone will see. Hoping someone will hear. Wishing you could disappear. Desperate for help you look around for a savior. Someone that will protect you from the horror that is about to occur.

No savior in sight only empty walls, closed doors and an end to what you finally thought was a peaceful life. Time goes by and you can't feel a thing. Your mind has gone from empty to lost.

What did I do? What did I say to deserve this pain? The only thing that rings in your head is, "Don't move. Don't scream. Don't give him a reason to be mean. Don't fight, just make it through the night." When it's all over, you thank God.

Pull yourself together! Straighten up this mess! If someone sees this place, they will easily guess! Clean yourself and wash your clothes! This way no one knows. All the while you replay the scenes in your head immediately wishing that you were dead.

How do you live with this? How do you go on? What if this happens to someone else? Others must be warned. Crazy you must be to think that you can tell! Telling will only make your life a living nightmare. The questions of "How?" The questions of "Who?" The questions of "What did they do?" Relive it over and over again for someone else to comprehend! Knowing full well that being scared to this degree is something they may never see. They'd tell you about how sorry they were. They would say they understood. Their understanding would do you no good. To truly under-stand you must be in it, you have to live through it.

Being scared for a few minutes is easy to endure. Being scared for years is torture. Scared to look people in the face. Scared to trust and watching their every move. Scared to get close to anyone. Scared of hugs and kisses. Scared that this secret will one day be divulged. For secrets can bring you a lifetime of pain. Secrets make you lose, not gain. Secrets will keep you in dark-ness and away from light. With every secret, there is a price.

It's time to live and now your secrets must be revealed. Don't think about the questions that will come. Don't think about the answers you will need to give. Just think about when it's all over how you will now be able to live. Live freely! Love freely! Not caring anymore about what others think or say. Just love them anyway. In those times of doubt and you feel yourself fading out, go to God's word and meditate on, *"The Lord is my light and my salvation; whom shall I fear? The Lord is the strength of my life; of whom shall I be afraid?"*[2]

Scared is a feeling that can be explained in so many differ-ent ways. Each person has their own definition of scared as it pertains to their life. If you take any of the feelings described in this book and tailor it to your own life, your interpretation will be totally different from mine. My job in these writings is not to get you to identify with how I feel as much as it is for you to begin to identify with your own feelings, so you can begin releasing what you may have allowed yourself to nurture in your spirit. I want to help you release those feelings that you have allowed yourself to hold on to, keeping you from having a full and wonderful life. If I do nothing else by sharing my life with you throughout the pages of this book, I hope to let you experience some of these feeling without having to live through them. I've always believed that you can learn from other people's life experiences. If I can help one person avoid living with thirty-something years or even one day of horror and regret, then I have fulfilled my purpose.

> Brethren, I count not myself to have apprehended: but this one thing I do, forgetting those things which are before, I press toward the mark for the prize of the high calling of God in Christ Jesus.
>
> (PHILIPPIANS 3:13–14, KJV)

This chapter, along with *Stolen*, was the one I was horrified to write. Then I realized that this writing explains itself. There is little else to add if it is read correctly because this one speaks for itself. Those who have been through something as devastating as rape on one occasion in their life is blessed because they have only experienced it once; unlike myself who has lived through several instances of rape, all by people I knew. They all claimed to care for me in some way, but caring for someone does not give you the right to violate someone's body.

The first time I was raped was when I was seventeen years old. My boyfriend at the time did not believe that I was not promiscuous, so he decided to prove it. While his sisters laughed in the living room, he dragged me through his house and into his bedroom where he accomplished his mission. The sad part about the whole thing is I was more worried about the fact that he would see I was not a virgin, unveiling the secret of my childhood. I didn't even care that he had taken my body unwillingly; I just wanted to make sure that my secret was not revealed.

The other times were during my adult life, and each time it had less of an affect on me. I was so numb to the whole ordeal by now that it would bother me for a day or so and then I was right back going about my daily routine, smiling and laughing. By this time I was so sick of the whole thing. I didn't want to live through another horrible memory or another ordeal. I didn't have room in my secret closet for any more baggage called *Scared*. I had bags and bags of scared all throughout my closet, and there just wasn't enough room to store anymore. Instead, I chalked it up to another bad experience and kept going.

During the last incident, I remember being a total mess. Not knowing whom else to call, I called a male friend of mine that I completely trusted and admired more than any man that I had known. Even though he was hundreds of miles away on his vacation, he stayed on the phone with me until I was calm and able to lie down and get some sleep. He suggested I call the police and press charges, but I told him that I couldn't. I didn't want to ruin my attacker's life. I knew that he had to raise and provide for his children. He did not question it, and he did not ridicule me for my decision. I thanked God for placing a man in my life that truly cared about me as a person and as a friend. He was someone that did not expect anything from me other than my friendship. Men like him are rare, so I count it an honor to have known him. By the next day, I had made up in my mind to count it as another day gone badly. It was over, so it was time to find something else to focus my time on.

Have you noticed a pattern? Think back on the other chapters. Do you remember me constantly saying something like: "I just let it go," "I chalked it up to ... " or "I buried it"? Do you see the pattern? I was constantly refusing to deal with the issues in my life; instead, I just hid them away for no one to see. I hid them under my smiles, my laughter, my singing, and my praise and worship. I was a walking lie. Everything about me was a lie. I smiled and laughed, but I wasn't happy. I sang, but my soul was empty and lonely. I continually went to church and participated in praise and worship, yet my heart was heavy.

It was during my brokenness before God that He revealed my purpose. In doing so, he also revealed to me that in order for Him to use me and to use me effectively I had to finally confront my past. I could not be effective in His kingdom and in the ministry He has put inside of me, holding on to secrets. I was in bondage to secrets and lies; it was time to let them all out of the closet. It was time for some house cleaning. I realized that I had to empty out that chest full of old clothes I no longer could fit. He equipped me with the only supplies I would ever need: His word. However, I had to be willing to use them. And guess what? I'm using them right now. This book *is* my housecleaning.

I will probably never be as raw or as open about my life

as I am right now; yet, I am the happiest I have ever been. I've found that it is okay to disagree with people and let your feelings be known as long as it's done with tact and not in anger. I've learned that I am allowed to have feelings and emotions without the fear of someone seeing and taking advantage of me. The biggest lesson of all was learning to love myself more than anyone else. By doing so, I have no problem saying "No" to people and things that are not healthy for my family or me. My closets are clean and the old things have been thrown away. I've started filling all this new space with fresh, godly things. By using God's cleaning supplies, He's showed me how to store up love, peace, joy, patience, temperance, and meekness.

Wash me thoroughly from mine iniquity, and cleanse me from my sin. For I acknowledge my transgressions: and my sin is ever before me. Against thee, thee only, have I sinned, and done this evil in thy sight: that thou mightest be justified when thou speakest, and be clear when thou judgest. Behold, I was shapen in iniquity; and in sin did my mother conceive me. Behold, thou desireth truth in the inward parts: and in the hidden part thou shalt make me to know wisdom. Purge me with hyssop, and I shall be clean: wash me, and I shall be whiter than snow. Make me to hear joy and gladness; that the bones which thou hast broken may rejoice. Hide thy face from my sins, and blot out all mine iniquities. Create in me a clean heart,

O God; and renew a right spirit within me. Cast me not away from thy presence; and take not thy Holy Spirit from me. Restore unto me the joy of thy salvation; and uphold me with thy free spirit. Then will I teach transgressors thy ways; and sinners shall be converted unto thee.

(PSALM 51:2–13, KJV)

What's in your closet? Is it time for you to clean house? Remember, before you can clean house you must first be ready and able to see all that you have stored away. If you're not willing to see what you have, then you won't be able to see what you need to rid yourself of. Aren't you tired of having to keep that closet door shut so that no one can take a peek? If you use the same cleaning supplies that I used, God's word, readily applying them to the really soiled areas, you can open your closet doors freely.

Depression

A state of feeling sad; a psychoneurotic or psychotic disorder marked especially by sadness, inactivity, difficulty in thinking and concentration, a significant increase or decrease in appetite and time spent sleeping, feeling of dejection and hopelessness, and sometimes suicidal tendencies.[1]

DEPRESSION

Pills on the nightstand waiting to be taken. Tears running down my face ready to relieve the pain. Desperation fills me as I try to figure out what to do. Tired of disappointment. Tired of living what seems to be a game that I never win. This one step will bring it to an end. No more fussing and fighting. No more unhappy feelings that I can't explain.

Everyday it's a battle to get out of bed. Having to go to work with a smile on my face knowing inside that my soul is hollow and dead. Smile and treat everyone with respect. I wish they all knew about my life of regret. Five days a week I dawn that fake smile. Thank

God it's Friday! Almost home! I just need to make it those last few miles.

Car parked, kids in their room. Away I go to my dungeon of gloom. In my bed I begin to dwell on how my life was supposed to go. Sleep will help me forget my sorrow. Oh my God I forgot about tomorrow. No work to take my mind off all the personal things. Twenty hours of sleep, what a relief. Here comes Sunday; same routine as yesterday. Another twenty hours of sleep, oh my goodness this is a little to deep.

Children knocking at the door, checking to see if I'm okay. I almost forgot. Have I seen them today? The look in their eyes says, "We're scared. What's wrong, Mommy? Is everything okay?" I say to myself, "What are you doing? You can't be a good mother. You might as well pick up those pills and write out your will."

Who will I give the children to? Who will I leave my letter for? What will my children say? Will they think that I didn't love them enough to stay? How could I leave and give them away? Will they ask someone, "Was it something they did? Was it something they said?" Will the person I leave them with love them and keep them safe? Will they care for them like I did? Will they treat them differently because they're not their kids?

No way out and no end in sight. God, this can't be from you. I don't know what to do. My life is a living hell. Turn on the TV and watch another movie. As my fingers scroll through the channels, I stumble across a message. A message of faith and hope for tomorrow! I continue to watch as tears stream down my face, and I finally realize that it's never too late. Someone loves me in spite of my issues. Someone cares enough to say, *"I will never leave thee, nor forsake thee!"*[2] I jump out of bed and head for the shower. For it's a new day and a new hour. Walk over to the nightstand and throw those pills away! God is watching over me, and all I need to do is pray. I haven't really prayed in years. Let's start off with something they taught me as a kid, *"The Lord is my shepherd; I shall not want. He maketh me to lie down in green pastures; he leadeth me beside the still waters. He restoreth my soul: he leadeth me in the paths of righteousness for his name's sake. Yea, though I walk through the valley of the shadow of death, I will fear no evil: for thou art with me; thy rod and thy staff they comfort me. Thou preparest a table before me in the presence of mine emenies: thou anointest my head with oil; my cup runneth over. Surely goodness and mercy shall follow me all the days of my life: and I will dwell in the house of the Lord for ever."*[3]

Depression is an emotion that is easy to disguise. We see thousands of people during the course of a week's time. Many people, when you look at them, look happy with no cares in the world. Underneath many of those brilliant costumes, used to disguise who they truly are, there are some who have layers and layers of loneliness, emptiness and even the feeling of being lost. Some may have lost a loved one; some may have been abused; some may have lost everything they have. Yet, there are still some that simply may not know *how* to live happy. How do you become something you've never been?

Well, you are reading the words of one of the masters of disguise. Those who know me will be totally surprised that I have lived a life of total depression. There have been numerous occasions when people I am in close contact with have complimented me on my friendly smile, my bubbly personality, and my energetic attitude. All of these compliments were indeed true because being surrounded by people that didn't know about my frustrations made me happy. I was always happy to not be home where the "real me" existed. Underneath all of those happy feelings I portrayed throughout the day, there was another layer that showed up right around the time I entered my home after work. It was that layer of emotion that made me not want to meet new people outside of my job. It was that layer that did not want to go anywhere, only to bed so I could forget about everything. It was that layer of depression that caused me not to want to eat.

Depression is a very dangerous thing. It will cause you to forget there are other people in your life, those that care about you. You stop answering the phone. You ignore the doorbell when people try to get in contact with you. You begin to avoid people in public. You search frantically for a quiet place off to the side where you hope that others will forget that you are even there. It will make you think that if you get into bed, ball up in a knot, and sleep the day away, you don't have to face the issues that are causing your misery. Well, I'm sorry to tell you that depression, almost like drinking and drugs, can become addictive. If you have enough of it then it will help you forget the pain—or so you think. Sadly, the issues will still be there when the high is over.

I always believed if you forgot the issue long enough, it would eventually go away. The pain and the emotions would eventually end. To some extent it did go away. It went from a surface problem to a buried problem that only resurfaced when someone or something triggers it. You deal with it, and then you bury it again. You eventually become a grave-yard of dead emotions. One day you look up and you're emotionless to the issues and the people around you. You stop caring about other people's problems. All you want is for them to go away and leave you alone.

Depression, if not conquered quickly, will get you to the point where life has no meaning. You will reach the height of the emotion—contemplating death. Considering death starts off as a *possible* solution; then, that *possible* solution turns into a *positive* one. That positive solution will then lead you to begin a plan of action. That plan of action will lead to preparation and preparation will lead you to D-day. Okay, D-day is death day in case I was about to lose any-body. This is the day you have to make the ultimate deci-sion: to choose life or death. Remember the choice is yours and only yours. Is ending your life worth it? Imagine never opening your eyes again. Imagine never seeing another sun rise or sunset. Imagine never seeing your children grow up and marry or even seeing your grandchildren. Imagine never living long enough to see what's on the other side of that problem.

I could be ashamed to admit to contemplating suicide

over four dozen times; but I have nothing to be ashamed about. Depression is a very serious emotion that happens more often than many people are willing to admit. Besides, I could never take that final step. There was always my worry of who would raise my children and how my action could possible destroy their lives. My cowardly action would cost them their livelihood. I had to remember that my life was not my own any longer. I had the responsibility of four children that depended on me as their mother to raise and protect them. How could I protect them if I was no longer around? How could I care for them if they never saw me again? How could I nurture them into adulthood if I was dead before they reached eighteen? I refused to be a coward and quit. That would mean that something got the best of me, and I was not about to let that happen.

Years before I gave my life to Christ, I used to pray that he would help me. I didn't know Him as my Savior, but I knew who He was and I loved Him even then. I used to tell Him that I knew He had a better life for me, better than the one I was living. I used to pray He would get me out of my marriage. I knew what marriage was supposed to be; therefore, I knew that my marriage was not His best for me. I used to pray for no more pain and misery. There were so many occasions I thought He did not hear me, or that He did not care. How could He if I was still living my life in hell?

The very last time I reached the height of my depression was several years ago. I would spend all of my free time in bed. I would park my car in the driveway on Friday evening and it would not move again until Monday morning when I left for work. A typical weekend for me would be me getting in bed as soon as I got home on Friday evening. I would get up long enough to take a shower and feed the children, not getting out of bed again until Saturday morning. I would wake up around six o'clock in the morning, have my morning coffee, and then I would sleep again until around ten or eleven. Then I would get up, shower and make the children "their second breakfast." I called it their second breakfast because they would get up on their own early in the morning and eat cereal, then wait patiently until I got up and fixed them a real breakfast. After breakfast, I would lay in bed until around five or six o'clock in the evening, sleeping or watching television. Eventually, I'd cook dinner, then back to bed I would go until the next morning. The next day would produce the exact same schedule, except Sunday would be my cleaning day. Now that I think about it, as depressed as I was, I refused to have a dirty house. My philosophy was that if I were going to end my life, neither the police nor anyone else would come into a dirty house—that I would be sure of! You may think it's funny, but you know how people talk when they go into another person's home and it's a complete mess.

Anyway, back on the subject. This went on over the course of a couple of months when one day, as I was lying in bed, I thought I should end my life—again. In my mind I was mapping out what I would do and how I would do it. In my head I was going through all of my relatives trying to think of whom I would give my children to. I had to come up with someone that would take care of them out of love, not just for the insurance money or the social security that they would get. As I was thinking, my son Demetrias came into my room to check on me as he always does. That day was different from all the others because this time when I looked at him I saw fear in his eyes as he asked me if there was anything he could get for me. I don't think I could ever describe the feeling that went through me as he walked out of the room. I felt like the worse mother in the entire world. I had to ask myself if I even knew what I was doing. What in the world would make me ever think to give my children up for someone else to raise? I scrapped the idea of ending my life that very day.

Days later, the depression was still there as I flipped through the television channels. I came across a channel with someone preaching the Word of God. I laid in bed listening to the message, and when the program ended, I felt a little better. I jumped out of bed and began doing things around the house. Over the course of several months it became a routine to watch different pastors on television. I would not even turn my television on until seven o'clock when Bishop T.D. Jakes' program, "The Potter's House," came on. There was always something in his messages that pierced my soul like no other. I found hope for the first time in my life. I began to change as I listened to him.

The more I listened, the more I realized it was time for me to turn my life around; but I didn't want to do like I used to when I lived at home. Back then I would give my life to Christ and within weeks turn back into the world.

I called my mother one night, (who I think is an awesome woman of God) to talk to her about giving my life to Christ. I remember telling her I knew I needed to give my life to Christ, but I wasn't sure how. I did not want to give my life to Him and then turn away the minute He fixed everything wrong in my life. I wanted to make sure that this time when I gave my life to Him it was forever. I told her I believed that my purpose was to minister to battered and abused women. I did not go through all the things I'd gone through in my life for nothing. When I spoke those words to her, my mother did not know the horrible trauma I'd gone through in my life in its entirety. She had no idea about everything in my life. Those were always areas that I refused to share with her because I wanted to protect her. I didn't know then that this book would be how I would minister not only to battered and abused women, but also to anyone looking for deliverance. She talked to me about turning my life over to God, allowing Him to use me in the areas that I talked to her about. She told me that I would know when I was ready and that would be when I turned my life over to Christ. I gave my life to Christ in May 2004, seven months after my brother passed away. My life has never been the same since.

I chose to live, not die. I chose to fight through the issues of life to see my existence turn out for the better because I knew that God had all the answers. I was finally willing to giving Him a chance. I had nothing else to lose.

I call heaven and earth to record this day against you, that I have set before you life and death, blessing and cursing: therefore choose life, that both thou and thy seed may live. That thou mayest love the Lord thy God, and that thou mayest obey his voice,

and that thou mayest cleave unto him: for
he is thy life, and the length of thy days:
that thou mayest dwell in the land which the
Lord sware unto thy fathers, to Abraham, to
Isaac, and to Jacob, to give them.

(DEUTERONOMY 30:19–20, KJV)

I don't know about you, but I plan to stick around to receive the many blessings God has for me. Wouldn't you love to be an heir to the promises of God? Can you fathom a life of fulfillment without one depressing day creeping up to bring you down? I'm not going to tell you every situation will be easy, but under the covering of the Lord you can get through them with a level of peace, knowing that whatever happens it will work out for your good in the end.

FRANCES A. OUTLAW

Emptiness

Containing nothing; not occupied or inhabited; lacking reality, substance, meaning or value.[1]

EMPTINESS

Empty hole that echoes in the night. Even if you look closely there is no light. At the end of the tunnel is only a body of bones. Your heart has turned into a pile of stone. Empty is your mind because it knows only pain. Empty is your soul because you have nothing to gain.

Empty is your smile. Empty is your laughter. Emptiness is why your life is such a disaster. Emptiness is what you feel when you turn the key at night knowing that emptiness is all that will be in sight. Emptiness is how you feel when you become the fifth wheel. Emptiness has no friends. It knows no joy. It has only sorrow. Emptiness is that feeling in the pit of your stomach that always keeps showing up when you think about the love that has died. It's even how you feel when the wrong someone declares their love and desire.

As you continue to live, the tunnel of emptiness just keeps getting covered—buried away in a deserted land. An image of what looks like joy and happiness catches your eyes. You run towards it in hopes of filling your cup and quenching your thirst. The closer you get the smaller it seems. Then you realize it was all just a dream. Did you expect to find joy? Did you expect to find peace? Let's be real; that was far beyond your reach.

Have you ever known joy? Have you ever known peace? Down the same lonely road you keep traveling. Looking for something in the distance. Looking for someone passing by. All that awaits you is a deserted wasteland waiting for you to drop to your knees and give up. As you travel along, you come across what you think is a mirage. It's the image of a man that hovers and not stands. With light all around Him, He cries, *"If any man thirst, let him come unto me, and drink. He that believeth on me, as the scripture had said, out of his belly shall flow rivers of living water."*[2]

If you were ask the reasoning behind the empty feeling a number of people experience in their lives, I am sure you could compile a long list of things. If people were honest with themselves, they would admit that emptiness is a feeling they themselves have developed. It is that part of ourselves that we are not happy with that causes us to feel empty. I can take any one of the emotions I described in this book to blame my emptiness on, but what it all boils down to is me. No one person or thing created the emptiness

FRANCES A. OUTLAW

inside of me. Instead of dealing with difficult situations as they occurred, I allowed them to build up inside of me, thus creating the negative images in my head and the emptiness in my soul.

> (For the weapons of our warfare are not carnal, but mighty through God to the pulling down of strong holds:) Casting down imaginations, and every high thing that exalteth itself against the knowledge of God, and bringing into captivity every thought to the obedience of Christ.

> (2 CORINTHIANS 10: 4–5, KJV)

God knew us from the foundation of the world. He instilled in us everything that we needed to fulfill His purpose for our lives. What we do or don't do with what He has given us is, in the end, up to us. It took me giving my life to Christ to realize that the emptiness that I have felt over the years came from my unwillingness to deal with issues from my past and my unwillingness to let go of those issues. I constantly found the need to hold on to the dead things, prohibiting me from getting any further in life. I hid in my closet full of secrets so I wouldn't have to develop any kind of normal relationship with my own family or friends. Hiding behind my problems allowed me to blame my emptiness on the falsehood that no one really cared about me or saw me for who I really was. When, in fact, I didn't care about myself.

Every time I allowed someone or something to dictate my life and my emotions, I created another empty spot in my soul. It may sound crazy to you, but think about the things that may have caused you to feel empty. Was it really whatever happened to you that caused your emptiness, or was it the decision you made based on your emotion that caused the emptiness? If you are honest with yourself, I bet you will say it was your emotion. The emotion that you felt is what caused you to handle the situation the way you did, leaving a big void in that area of your life.

When will we stop letting people and things decide for us? When will we take the time to learn who God says that we are and what we can have? How do we find out what and who is best for us when we have not gone to the one that knows us better than we know ourselves?

Do you know who you are? Do you know what you do and do not like? What makes you happy? Have you learned to be happy alone? Have you learned that you are so special that you do not have to wait on anyone else to cater to your needs? God said in His word that He has predestined your life, so why don't you ask the one that knows your life from the beginning to the end? Don't look to man to tell you who or what you can have, but seek the God that has your history already written. Ask God what His plan and purpose is for your life. Ask Him to reveal the real you to you. When you ask Him, make sure you are prepared for the person that He will show you in the mirror. All of it may not be good, but it will help you develop a change in yourself for the better if you are sincere. As He begins to show you, watch the masks you have worn for so many years start disappearing.

Always remember this: People will only see you the

way that you see yourself. I know you have heard this a thousand times already, but when will you let it sink in? Allowing yourself to hide under camouflage will never give people the opportunity to see the real you. How can you develop a relationship with anyone hiding under your facade? When will you let them get to know the person under the layers? It is time to open that closet door, pull out all of your hidden faces and begin to unmask them all. That emptiness you feel inside is coming from the fact that all of the real parts of you are hidden in your secret closet covered in masks of all different shapes and sizes. There are the small ones from today and the large ones from your past. It's time to unveil the masks. Let God guide you to your liberation. Are you ready for deliverance?

NOTES

Purpose

1. Holy Bible, King James Version–*Romans 3:23*

Who Am I?

1. Merriam Webster Collegiate Dictionary–(www.merriamwebster.com)
2. Merriam Webster–(www.merriamwebster.com)
3. Merriam Webster–(www.merriamwebster.com)
4. Merriam Webster–(www.merriamwebster.com)

Lost

1. Merriam Webster–(www.merriamwebster.com)
2. Holy Bible, King James Version - *Matthew 18:11*

Loneliness

1. Merriam Webster–(www.merriamwebster.com)
2. Holy Bible, King James Version–*Matthew 7:7–8*

Stolen

1. Merriam Webster–(www.merriamwebster.com)
2. Holy Bible, King James Version–*John 10:10*

Fighting

1. Merriam Webster–(www.merriamwebster.com)
2. Holy Bible, King James Version–*Ephesians 6:13*
3. Holy Bible, King James Version–*Proverbs 4:23*

Struggle

1. Merriam Webster–(www.merriamwebster.com)
2. Holy Bible, King James Version–*Romans 5:3–6*

Hurt

1. Merriam Webster–(www.merriamwebster.com)
2. Holy Bible, King James Version–*1 Corinthians 9:24*
3. Holy Bible, King James Version–*Psalm 30:5*

Scared

1. Merriam Webster–(www.merriamwebster.com)
2. Holy Bible, King James Version–*Psalm 27:1*

Depression

1. Merriam Webster–(www.merriamwebster.com)
2. Holy Bible, King James Version–*Hebrews 13:5*
3. Holy Bible, King James Version–*Psalm 23*

Emptiness

1. Merriam Webster–(www.merriamwebster.com)
2. Holy Bible, King James Version–*John 7:37–38*

listen|imagine|view|experience

AUDIO BOOK DOWNLOAD
INCLUDED WITH THIS BOOK!

In your hands you hold a complete digital entertainment package. Besides purchasing the paper version of this book, this book includes a free download of the audio version of this book. Simply use the code listed below when visiting our website. Once downloaded to your computer, you can listen to the book through your computer's speakers, burn it to an audio CD or save the file to your portable music device (such as Apple's popular iPod) and listen on the go!

How to get your free audio book digital download:

1. Visit www.tatepublishing.com and click on the e|LIVE logo on the home page.
2. Enter the following coupon code:
   1281-761d-456b-49d0-e238-e559-db0a-87a6
3. Download the audio book from your e|LIVE digital locker and begin enjoying your new digital entertainment package today!